The House of Your Dream

The House of Your Dream

AN INTERNATIONAL COLLECTION OF PROSE POETRY

Edited by
ROBERT ALEXANDER & DENNIS MALONEY

Introduction by
PETER JOHNSON

WHITE PINE PRESS / BUFFALO, NEW YORK

Published by
White Pine Press
P.O. Box 236   Buffalo, New York 14201
www.whitepine.org

Acknowledgments begin on page 191.

Publication of this book was made possible, in part, with public funds from the New York State Council on the Arts, a State Agency.

First Edition

ISBN 978-1-893996-98-4

Printed and bound in the United States of America

Cover art: Detail from "Embroidering the Earth's Mantle" by Remedios Varo (1908–1963). Oil on Masonite, 1961.

Library of Congress Control Number: 2008929956

The Marie Alexander Poetry Series, Volume 11.

Editors' Note

When the time came to discuss a project that would celebrate the 35th anniversary of the founding of White Pine Press, we began to contemplate an anthology drawn from all the books that White Pine has published through the years. It didn't take long for us to see the folly of such an endeavor, as it would take more time and energy, and more pages, than we had available. We listened, at that point, to the advice we recalled from our earliest writing classes: Limit your topic. And given the predilection we both feel for the magical form that is the prose poem, it didn't take long for us to conceive of a prose poem anthology drawn from all the books that White Pine has published (or will soon publish) in its variegated career. We think it's a fitting tribute to all the individuals—writers, editors, funders, and of course readers—who have helped White Pine survive these many years. Many thanks to you all. We couldn't have done it without you.

—The Editors

THE HOUSE OF YOUR DREAM

I enter your house with stealth, making sure I'm dressed properly—checking buttons, the shine on my shoes—trying to look normal because you say your dreams are so ordinary and I don't want to stand out. You say you spend your dreams packing and shopping, engaging in small talk. But inside your dream I notice a strange light, the light that colored your childhood, and your suitcases are covered with exotic stickers. The very streets you windowshop along are unlike any streets I remember—each store a museum of the mysterious, each window faceted like a diamond. I follow a few paces behind you as you buy tea and apples—the tea seems alive with the sounds of India and each apple has a window where families look out and wave. Each object you meet glows with that old light, even the sidewalk looks like a rainbow—because it is your dream and I am a stranger here.

—Vern Rutsala

Contents

Introduction

About twenty years ago we prose poets lived in relative obscurity, lucky if we could get editors to read, much less publish, our work. This fact became clear to me after I founded *The Prose Poem: An International Journal* and received letter after letter from prose poets who felt the journal authenticated their poetry in some way. For sure, books of prose poems had been published before that time but they were usually written by established verse poets, who frequently, and quite strangely, either apologized for writing prose poems or called them something else.

Back then there were also short-term projects or special issues that kept us hoping for another prose poem renaissance, like the one that occurred in the late '60s and early '70s when so many of us kept trying to preserve our copies of Michael Benedikt's *The Prose Poem: An International Anthology*, which had the worst glue binding of any book ever published. We all also had our own private histories with the genre, coming to it from many different angles, sometimes from writers in Benedikt's anthology, other times through related genres like the Chinese *fu*, the aphorism, and the fairy tale or parable. I became interested in writing short prose after translating Theophrastus' character sketches and reading Kafka and Novalis. But my history with the prose poem was also very much tied to White Pine Press, even before I began publishing with them.

Dennis Maloney and Elaine LaMattina, editorially, have always been ahead of the game. They published poetry from abroad before it was hip to do so: anthologies of poetry and fiction from Canada, Latin America, Eastern Europe, and Asia, and their "Secret Weavers Series," "Korean Voices Series," "Companions for the Journey Series," and "Terra Incognita Series" series have spawned such contemporary prose-poem classics as Aleš Debeljak's *Anxious Moments*. One of my favorite White Pine prose-poem books is Pablo Neruda's *The House in the Sand*. Even as early as 1985, White Pine Press made a commitment to prose poetry by publishing Louis Jenkins's *The Water's Easy Reach*—this when Jenkins was relatively unknown.

It seems appropriate, then, even predestined, that White Pine Press and Robert Alexander partnered up. Alexander was himself aligned for years with Bill Truesdale's New Rivers Press, which has always favored publishing books of prose poems, and Alexander, along with Mark Vinz and Truesdale, edited the ground-breaking *The Party Train: An Anthology of North American Prose Poetry* in 1995. Later Alexander founded the Marie Alexander Poetry Series, which White Pine Press is now publishing.

   This anthology presents the riches of all their efforts, plus poems from *The Best of the Prose Poem: An International Journal,* which White Pine Press published as a book in 2000. You probably couldn't find three sensibilities more different than Alexander's, Maloney's, and mine. Maloney, who has always favored the deep image, surrealistic Latin American prose poem, has enlarged the margins of the genre with his interest in Korean and Slovenian poetry. Alexander has been a long-time devotee of the nature prose poem made famous by Robert Bly, but his recent choices for the Marie Alexander series have included Morton Marcus's parables, Marie Harris's lyrical essays, and Lawrence Millman's meditations. I'll leave a description of my tastes to someone else, but I hope an interesting recent history of the prose poem emerges in the following pages. There are poems from poets from the first renaissance (Bly, Wright, Benedikt, Edson, Simic, and Marcus); poems from poets of the second renaissance (Lombardo, Koncel, Andrews, Liotta, Clary, and Young); and then there is the newer generation led by Peter Conners. But influences from abroad are everywhere: poems by Char, Jacob, Ponge, Follain, Mistral, Mah, Oravecz, and others.

   I've often wondered what makes a good anthology. Obviously you need good poems. But an absence of ego also helps. Over the years Maloney and Alexander have labored separately and quietly outside the moneyed resources of academia to pursue their own personal visions. The prose poem brought them together, and, with this anthology, we are fortunate to enjoy the fruits of that marriage.

—Peter Johnson

The House of Your Dream

Samuel Ace

Prayer

*(I started to write & the letter upset me & I called
and cried & you washed the sheets & had me pray.)*

So you said and yes I like lipstick not on me on you you cried on the phone
overwhelmed by my love and yours by all the too many words by your days
which go by now too fast with too much work and not enough time by your
cold by and for desire you cried in your home sitting in your blue plaid
chair next to the low table low chair and the couch we made love on which
now holds your lover passed out on dark wine you cried and asked if I was
sleeping upstairs tonight you cried because I said no because I said I washed
the sheets and tried to tell you why: I woke this morning upstairs in the
guest room where you slept with me which is my room really as it holds my
books my rain man kachina my volcano my fertility my rocks I slept there
the night before (Monday) and the night before that (Sunday) which was
the day you drove off into the dark I slept there because I did not want to
lose you but I woke hot and dry from the woodstove I woke wanting to for-
get you were far away again to forget that when I went to sleep I held you
in my mind and felt you hold me but also felt the shadow of your lover next
to you I woke thinking it was time to sleep in a cooler place time to sleep
in the bed downstairs where I had slept for five years with my lover to sleep
on the side of the bed I chose near the window for quick escape and to look
out at the weather (the only windows upstairs I needed and had were your
mouth and the fragrant dawn of your hair) I woke and intended to sleep
downstairs my back turned to the wide expanse of the bed to wake up and
to look out at my pine tree and the empty bird feeder and everything that
was safe and everything that kept me separate and alone

The night you called and cried I did sleep downstairs but before I slept I
also prayed and I prayed again when I got up and like you I rose in the dawn
freed and in love and in the new morning you said (on the phone again)
Look but don't touch and for the first time claimed me for your own.

Kim Addonizio

Last Gifts

They were gathered in the room next to the kitchen, where he had his hospital bed cranked up. A writer he had published brought him a long red boa and draped it around his neck; he looked like someone drowning, a small head floating on feathery waves. Someone else brought a pillow stitched with a picture of Elvis, with the words "King of Rock and Roll" across the top. There were red splotches on his arms, and his hand shook slightly when he poured water into the glass on his tray. A poet took a book off the crowded shelves, sat on the edge of the bed and read to him for a while. Someone accidentally stood on the oxygen hose; no one noticed until he began to cough, and there was some consternation, and then relieved laughter and joking. The party grew more animated; people refilled their drinks, and everyone started talking at once. His wife went to the kitchen and brought back a big silver bowl of buttered popcorn and passed it around. For a few moments it seemed as though they had forgotten him. Then someone finished a story, someone else paused to think of the right word, and a silence opened and spread through the brightly lit room. The guests looked at each other; some had tears in their eyes. They turned to the bed, where the sick man sat smiling at them in his red boa, and he knew this was what it would be like when he was gone. And then he was.

—*for Al*

Robert Alexander

Only in Retrospect

It's only in retrospect that you can say, "This was the last warm day of the year"—sometime in early October, before the storm clouds come sweeping in across Lake Superior and the temperature drops twenty degrees in an hour. But yesterday was one such day, a mild wind blowing from the south, a few leaves dropping from the multi-colored trees.

More than a hundred crows flocked along the shore of Sable Lake, jawing back and forth into the morning air; two kingfishers flew upward into a cedar as I put my canoe into the water; out on the ruffled lake I saw a quintet of loons—flying south already?—and as I rounded the point near Towes Creek a bald eagle flew off from a maple and headed down the lake. Though the crows were all about, they hardly seemed to notice: a few made cursory passes toward the eagle but almost, it seemed, pro forma, cawing in mild dismay—nothing, to be sure, like the way they mobbed an owl roosting outside my bedroom window one morning last winter.

In the afternoon I took my dog up to the Sucker River, and as we approached the high banks a single raven across the valley took off and circled overhead. By then the wind had died (only hours later it had shifted to the north and was building toward thirty knots), and we could hear the river gurgling like a broken faucet beneath us. Before us and around us and across the valley the trees stood motionless in their red and orange party clothes. Having worked all summer to store up food, and having been released till spring from the need to make a living, they were at last free to lose their green and stand for all to see in their true, most personal finery.

After another week or two and a few more north winds, the revelry would be over and they would strip down and go to bed naked, to sleep it off beneath the winter's snows.

Old Possum

The only marsupial in North America. Five toes on each foot; inside toe on hind foot opposable (an aid in climbing) and without claw. . . . Among the most primitive of living mammals. . . . May live seven years or more.
—*Mammals* (Peterson Field Guides)

Here's how it happens. The night before the full moon (the air still mild in October), while Ralph is walking his dog and the moon's shadows play under the oaks, he sees up the block, beneath the sole streetlight, just as his dog comes alert, an animal about the size of a large cat, with a pointed nose—and then it's gone and Ralph's dog is whining and straining at the leash.

The next morning, from his canoe out on the water, Ralph sees a possum by the shore, standing on a rock, face pointed downward. As Ralph moves closer, he sees that the creature's head is nodding like an old man falling asleep in his chair. When his nostrils hit the water, small bubbles appear on the lake's surface and the possum jerks his head up. As Ralph moves even closer, the animal senses his presence and raises his head, and Ralph sees that he's blind, no eyes left in his sockets, and yet he seems to have a clear idea of just where Ralph is, and starts to back up, the prehensile thumbs on his rear feet gripping the slick rock, appearing to Ralph as worn and lumpy as his father's hands before he died.

Later that day, walking his dog, Ralph sees that the possum has lain down in the water and is curled up with his head on a small rock and the gentle waves lapping his fur. At first Ralph thinks he's dead, but once again the creature must sense Ralph's presence—or smells his dog—and slowly he gets to his feet and faces them. Ralph withdraws, keeping his dog close by him on the leash, and the possum lies back down. A late bloom of algae by the water's edge covers the lower half of the possum in a pale green.

That night the full moon spreads its quicksilver across the lake, and the air is still mild. The next day, when Ralph walks his dog, the wind is blowing out of the northwest and there's a chill in the air. When Ralph gets to the lake's edge, he sees the rocks are empty. In the night, Ralph imagines, beneath the soft canopy of the full moon, the possum rose like Elijah and, crossing the light-filled lake, ascended heavenward . . . while the autumn moon, a perfect circle of white, moved through the cloudless sky.

Agha Shahid Ali

Dear Shahid,

I am writing to you from your faroff country. Far even from us who live here. Where you no longer are. Everyone carries his address in his pocket so that at least his body will reach home.

Rumors break on their way to us in the city. But word still reaches us from border towns: Men are forced to stand barefoot in snow waters all night. The women are alone inside. Soldiers smash radios and televisions. With bare hands they tear our houses to pieces.

You must have heard Rizwan was killed. Rizwan: Guardian of the Gates of Paradise. Only eighteen years old. Yesterday at Hideout Cafe (everyone there asks about you), a doctor—who had just that morning treated a 16-year-old boy released from an interrogation center—said: *I want to ask the fortune tellers: Did anything in his line of Fate reveal that the webs of his hands would be cut with a knife?*

This letter, *insh'Allah*, will reach you, for my brother goes south tomorrow where he shall post it. Here one can't even manage postage stamps. Today I went to the post office. Across the river. Bags and bags—hundreds of canvas bags—all of undelivered mail. By chance I looked down and there on the floor I saw this letter addressed to you. So I am enclosing it. I hope it's from someone you are longing for news of.

Things here are as usual, though we always talk about you. Will you come soon? Waiting for you is like waiting for spring. We are waiting for the almond blossoms. And, if God wills, O! those days of peace when we all were in love and the rain was in our hands wherever we met.

Jack Anderson

Return to Work

I have returned to the job from which I was fired a whole decade ago. The funny thing is, no one recognizes me.

The same fat jolly bleached-blonde woman who was my department head then is my department head now. We get along well together. From the very first we share favorite jokes.

The same vice president who fired me then is vice president still. He is tall, skinny, nervous. He doesn't like my looks, he keeps lecturing me about duty. Yet he has to approve my appointment. What a bastard he is.

And there at their desks are all my pals from the old days: Bill, Carol, Russ, Al, Serena, David, Monty, and Cliff. Just as before.

And not one of them recognizes me. I have begun anew, totally anew.

Sometimes I think my fat blonde department head recognizes me. She smiles at me as though she's guessed my secret. But I know that's a subject she'll never bring up. Best of all, the skinny bastard vice president, though he may not like my looks, doesn't realize who I am.

So I sit at my desk as though I never sat there before. I sit there powerful in my secret knowledge. How wonderful.

I am a new man. How wonderful. How wonderful it is to return to work.

The Party Train

To bring joy and friendliness to the New York subway system, which is all too often bleak and indifferent, I propose that a special train be instituted to be known as The Party Train. Each day, this train would follow one or another of the city's existing routes, sometimes on the local, sometimes on the express tracks. No extra fare would be charged, the cars would be painted exactly the same as those of any other train, but inside there would be a perpetual party. The poles and straps would be festooned with streamers, and Japanese lanterns would hang from the ceiling. Food and drink would always be available, ranging from corned beef to caviar, from beer to champagne. Strolling musicians would roam from car to car. And the last car would be transformed into a gigantic bed where anyone could take a date, no questions asked.

The Party Train would not only be fun to ride, the very knowledge of its existence would be a source of cheer. For the route it would follow on any given day would never be announced in advance, but would always come as a fresh surprise. Thus any citizen waiting in any station could hope that the next train to pull in—accompanied by a shower of confetti and a whiff of pot smoke—would be The Party Train, so he could step aboard and glut himself on cashew nuts and kisses from the Battery to the Bronx. Or if he were in a local station and The Party Train happened to be an express that day, he could watch it rumble by, glimpsing paper hats and saxophones bouncing in the front cars and naked bodies flickering among the pillows at the back. Then he would chuckle to himself, glad that there was something interesting to look at while waiting for the subway, and wishing that tomorrow The Party Train might finally stop for him.

Nin Andrews

The Obsession

Occasionally the sailor suspects a woman swims nude beneath his ship, though when he dives into the water, he sees only white jellyfish opening and closing like umbrellas. He is reminded of the time when he was a boy and imagined ordinary stones were gems, lovely enough to win the heart of the girl next door. But he never reached to pick one up. Instead he decided the girl would never like him. The more he thought about her not liking him, the more he grew to despise her and her adolescent beauty. The more he despised her, the more he wanted to see her, to follow her, to sit just behind her, and never let her out of his sight. That was the beginning of the obsession. Evenings he stayed up late, peeking through his Venetian blinds, hoping to catch a glimpse of her in her pink striped pajamas. Every weeknight she stretched out on the lime green carpet in her living room and did her homework in front of the flickering TV. The boy began to believe that if he did not watch her, she might not do her homework. Then she might do poorly in school and be mocked, and he would have to protect her. What if he didn't know how? Better to be sure she did her work. But the more he stared at her, the more beautiful she became, the more her skin softened, and the silk of her hair awakened him from his dreams. He grew convinced his eyes gave off a kind of glow that polished the girl, like an apple, that she could never have been as lovely if he had not looked at her so intensely. He even thought his staring might have been making her breasts grow, just as the sun's heat caused fruit to ripen. That's when he realized her beauty was a kind of death wish. Like a mirage, he thought. A mirage of an oasis in the Sahara, something that could never satisfy his thirst. No wonder years later he still saw her breasts in the middle of the sea. No wonder he hated her.

In Grandma's Bathroom

Centipedes scurried up the stone wall, squeezing into the cracks. I'd stare into her broken mirror and at the row of empty cologne bottles. Her toilet never stopped running. Grandma would come in and rattle the handle, take the top off the tank, pull the black ball in the back, saying I wasn't supposed to be using the facilities in there anyhow. As if her huge, ancient behind made the pink porcelain seat unfit for my bony young one. One time Grandma sat on the toilet seat and broke it. Another time I came in and saw her, wrinkled and wet, rising up like a genie out of a bottle. There was so much of her, I couldn't stop staring and wondering how it all fit in one tub, on one set of bones. She dried off all that body with one small towel, saying, "Look here, Honey Child, don't you be slipping in here again, hear?"

Ruth Behar

Poem xxxv

I thought I would never hear a bird sing again. I thought the trees would forget how to grow leaves. The winter was too long. Too silent. The house fell dark and I could no longer tell the day from the night. I was certain our love had died. I wept and wept. I filled a box with my tears. They shone like pearls that once knew how to swim in the ocean.

Today all the windows are open. Since dawn the birds have been singing deliriously. The trees have turned crazy green. I can smell the flowers in my garden yielding their honey to the bees.

I never wanted a garden—

I did not plant the flowers, I do not know the names of the birds or the trees, yet their wild pleasure is not withheld from me.

How fortunate is the world that it does not depend on my will. How fortunate am I that you keep watering the stem of our love, even when it withers, even when it has nothing to give.

MICHAEL BENEDIKT

The Toymaker Gloomy
but Then Again Sometimes Happy

(I) How can a person practically drowning in the seas of circumstance, and beneath wave after wave of our usual, daily, dirty, diurnal dreck, possibly attempt to engage fulltime in the production of Magical Objects? That is, I think, a relatively simple question which perhaps virtually every person who prides himself on being both a serious craftsperson and a good citizen of our ordinary, everyday world must ask himself or herself every now and then. Good heavens!—just try waking up first thing in the morning with a few nice, clear Visions of Bliss in your head, and then try perambulating just a few blocks beyond the relative safety and calm of your own house or apartment—and just see how long your own otherwise probably quite cheery, creative, early-morning attitude survives even *that* little stroll into madness and disorder! Yes, if only as a form of minor mental exercise, just try calculating the exact effect that your own very first everyday encounters with the external world and the people in it exert upon you and your own, otherwise probably rather optimistic, fresh-as-a-daisy, early-morning disposition—and see then whether you really feel like going around all day long thinking playful, creative thoughts, chuckling pleasantly to yourself, and generally smiling and laughing! (2) I don't know how you feel about it, but for years and years, from the point of view of a person practicing my own, would-be benignly optimistic profession—that of a struggling manufacturer of colorful and sometimes even relatively amusing toys—I've felt that this constant placing of myself into bad moods by the conventional world, practically amounts to theft! Theft of my good moods, theft of my creative, inventive capacities—theft, even, of my precious peace-of-mind! Don't you, yourself, think that us serious craftspeople spend a whole lot more time than we should have to, defending ourselves against the incursions of a virtual slew of tedious mentalities, seemingly intent on slipping themselves into our mental or even actual billfolds? (3) Still, we press on! As a devoted Toymaker, for example, I for one know that I must! The children, after all, want to be entertained! The public is practically crying out for novelty! (4) And besides, there's at least one additional reason for those of us who happen to be Toymakers, for example, to press on: the fact is that Toymakers, too, sometimes get miserably bored! And so, occasionally (sometimes when we least expect it!), we feel the sudden urge to try to produce, in counter-response, a pretty doll with eyes sharp and bright enough to light up the world; or, sometimes, a stuffed teddy-bear which sings whimsical tunes—and which, every now & then, sometimes even dances. . . .

Robert Bly

Finding the Father

My friend, this body offers to carry us for nothing—as the ocean carries logs. So on some days the body wails with its great energy; it smashes up the boulders, lifting small crabs, that flow around the sides.

Someone knocks on the door. We do not have time to dress. He wants us to go with him through the blowing and rainy streets, to the dark house.

We will go there, the body says, and there find the father whom we have never met, who wandered out in a snowstorm the night we were born, and who then lost his memory, and has lived since longing for his child, whom he saw only once . . . while he worked as a shoemaker, as a cattle herder in Australia, as a restaurant cook who painted at night.

When you light the lamp you will see him. He sits there behind the door . . . the eyebrows so heavy, the forehead so light . . . lonely in his whole body, waiting for you.

The Orchard Keeper

We walk together through the new snow. No one has walked through it or looked at it. The deep snow makes the sound the porgies hear near the ocean floor, the hum the racer hears the moment before his death, the sound that lifts the buoyant swimmer in the channel.

Four pigeon grass stalks, scarce and fine, lift their heads above the snow. They are four heron legs moving in white morning fog, the musical thoughts that rise as the pianist sits down at her table, the body laboring before dawn to understand its dream.

In our dream, we walk along a stone wall, and pause at an open gate. We look in at an orchard where a fount of water is rising in the air. We see armed men lying asleep all around the fountain, each with his sword lying under him.

And the orchard keeper . . . where is he?

Paul Celan

IV

Once again I hang the big white umbrellas in the night air. I know, Columbus's new route doesn't lead this way, my archipelago will remain undiscovered. The endless ramifications of the aerial roots, from which I hang by one hand then the other, will embrace in solitude, unknown to the seekers of the heights, the hands will clutch more and more convulsively and will never again give up their gloves of melancholy. I know this, just as I know I can't trust the tides that, with foam churned up from the bottom, bathe the lacy shores of these islands which should belong to authoritarian sleep. Under my bare feet the sand begins to burn. I rise up on my toes and drift over there. I can't expect hospitality, I know that, too, but where should I stop if not over there? They don't receive me. An unknown messenger waits at sea to tell me every port is forbidden to me. I offer him my hands bleeding from the floating thorns of the nocturnal sky in exchange for a moment of rest, hoping that from the silky shore of my first parting from myself I can hoist up a row of billowing sails and continue my journey. I offer my hands to see that the equilibrium of this posthumous flora is preserved from danger. Once again I'm rejected. I have no choice but to keep traveling, but my strength is exhausted, and I close my eyes to look for a man with a boat.

VIII

There were nights when it seemed to me your eyes, under which I drew large orange dark bags, were about to ignite their ashes again. Those nights there was less rain. I would open the windows and climb, naked, onto the windowsill to look out at the world. The trees of the forest would march toward me, one by one, obedient, a defeated army come to lay down its arms. I stayed still, and the sky lowered its flag under which the armies fought. From one corner you watched me, too, as I stood there, beautifully bleeding in the nude: I was the only constellation extinguished by the rain, I was the Southern Cross. But those nights it was hard to open your veins when the flames covered me, the citadel of urns was mine, I filled it with my blood, after dismissing the enemy army, rewarding it with cities and harbors, and the silver panther tore up the dawns lying in wait for me. I was Petronius, and once again I was shedding my blood among the roses. For each stained petal you extinguished a torch.

Do you remember? I was Petronius, and I didn't love you.

Translated by Magda Carneci and Christopher Merrill.

René Char

You Did Well to Leave, Arthur Rimbaud

You did well to leave, Arthur Rimbaud! Your eighteen years as obstinate about friendship, ill will and the silliness of Paris poets as about the buzzing of that pointless bee, your slightly mad Ardennes family, you did well to throw them to the winds, hurl them under the blade of their own precocious guillotine. You had reason to abandon the lazy boulevard, the bars with their lousy poems, for the beastly underworld, for wily commerce, the happiness of halfwits.

That absurd stride of body and spirit, that bullet that whacks its target, makes it burst, yes, that's really where it's at, the life of a man! After leaving childhood, one can't forever throttle one's brother. What if volcanoes do change the place a little, and their lava, running through the world's great void, brings to it some qualities that sing among the wounds?

You did well to leave, Arthur Rimbaud! You got some of us wondering what luck we'd have if we did things your way.

The Lichens

I was walking among the ridges of a wasteland, amnesic plants, hushed breathing. The mountain loomed, a shadow-filled flask, assuming for the moment the gesture of thirst. My existence, all trace of me had disappeared. Your face receded before me. Only a bee searching for its spot would have called it living, made it flower. We were going to separate. You would live on the fragrant plateau and I would enter the garden of the void. There in the safekeeping of rocks, in the wind's fullness, I would ask the absolute night to dispose of my sleep in whatever way might make you happiest. And the fruits of our love would remain with you.

Translated by Susanne Dubroff.

Maxine Chernoff

The Sound

—I hate it when we have sex and you make that sound.

—What sound?

—The sound you make when you're about to have orgasm.

—What sound do you mean?

—I can't describe it. It sounds like no other sound you ever make.

—But why do you hate it?

—It scares me.

—Why would it scare you?

—I guess it's because we're at an intimate moment, and you make an unfamiliar sound.

—It must be my intimate-moment sound.

—But it doesn't sound intimate. It sounds . . . well . . . brutal.

—I make a brutal sound?

—Yes, I think that's how I'd describe it.

—Make the sound for me.

—I can't.

—Of course you can. You remember it, don't you?

—I'm embarrassed to make it.

—You're not embarrassed to tell me, but you're embarrassed to make it?

—Right.

—Just try.

—All right. It's something like "Yowwwwwohwoewoe."

—And that sounds brutal to you?

—It does.

—It sounds to me like I'm very happy.

—It doesn't sound happy to me.

—What sound would you like me to make?

—I don't have an alternative in mind. I just thought I'd tell you that the sound you make, well, it brings me out of the moment. Sex ends for me when I hear that sound.

—That's good, isn't it?

—Why is it good?

—Because you know I've had an orgasm when you hear it.

—But what if I want to do something more to you?

—More? We've both finished by then. What more would we do?

—What if I still want to kiss you and you're making that sound?

—Well, I guess you could try and see.

—Should I try now?

—Why do you think I want you to kiss me when you can't stand the sound I make at my most vulnerable moment?

—I didn't mean I couldn't stand it. I just meant it's distracting.

—Maybe you should gag me.

—Then you'd make the sound but it would be even worse.

—Why would it be worse?

—It would sound all mumbed and sad, like the voice of someone locked inside of a trunk.

—So, you'd rather I sound brutal than all muffled and sad?

—I guess so.

—You must really love me then.

KIM CHINQUEE

Big Cages

She slept with the tiger, touching his fur and resting on his shoulder. He was meaty and gentle, with big teeth that he only showed with a yawn. She woke from a dream about a burglar and felt the tiger's paw on her arm, and she questioned if there was a boy, her boy in the next room, who was really not a boy now. He was a man with a stuffed bear animal and the stuffed bear was getting up to use the bathroom. She looked at her tiger—she'd watched Discovery and that mirage, the circus, tigers in big cages, a man, a bear, a trapeze artist. She heard flushing from the bathroom. She started to get up to check if the bear was real and if she really had a son, or was he a boy or man now? She moved closer to the tiger and pulled herself under him like a blanket, hearing his heart thump evenly.

No One Was with Him

He had his own business and let himself off at five, like a regular employee, and every day afterwards he called her, and today when she asked him how his day was he said fine except for the accident. She said what accident and he said he rolled his truck a few times. She said are you ok and he said he was perfectly fine. He said his truck was probably totaled but he wouldn't find out for sure until the weekend. She cradled the phone and asked if he was scared and he said he didn't have time to be scared and she said, but weren't you? At all? Like, didn't you have a moment of freakiness and he said no. He'd slipped his truck on ice, whirling and spinning, rolling one, two, he wasn't sure how many times, and she said was your brother with you? Maybe your new puppy? No one was with him. Someone called 911 and it had happened in the morning and she kept asking more questions that he didn't seem to want to answer and she picked up a fork from the table and started unraveling the hem of her dress and kept asking him what now? and what if? and he said he was fine, he was perfectly fine and then she started ripping her dress and took it off and she got up and looked at herself in the mirror, the phone the only thing on her and her hair was bedraggled, her make-up ran and she tried to remember the last time he even touched her or if he even would again and she said please and are you sure that you're ok and he said he was fine, he was perfectly fine, Hun, he was perfectly fine with everything.

KILLARNEY CLARY

Clear of oak groves, sunrise stretched a thin reach deep into the chamber, tripping the setting of fires on hilltops: signals relayed to the quarters. A day to plant or hunt, enter women or agreements.

Night skies were laid on fields in perfect orientation before the plates opened, wandered, collided; they continue and will. There is so much to take into account. It may be impossible to choose for myself; all pleasures might hand me loneliness.

I'll find the dark room, tip the white table to catch a shaft bent by a mirror, shot through a pin hole, and I'll watch the ocean upside down. Foam churns at the edge of a vision. It is time to do something in particular.

Early radios talk about traffic and weather as if they vary. People phone in with opinions on the metrorail and stories of most embarrassing moments, and it's slow through the interchange until I glide up onto the ten heading west. I dreamt Russ came to me scared, said he couldn't stop the rainstorm in his mouth.

In another sleep he was a wizard with crescents and stars on a tall hat; this afternoon at lunch he tells me we are made of waves and there is no time. Before we meet again I will forget his face; I will reassign meanings to what we've said.

I stand in the yard tonight; the reflection of the full moon scribbles on the surface of the tea I drink. Instead of figuring it, I watch the figuring; I catch my desire to have it still. Maybe there isn't any code to break.

A Man Learns to Fly

In his younger years his father had toted him out to the bird feeder. It was brown, bent, speckled with white droppings—angled against all seasons. No mix was sufficient to keep the lesser birds away: Old bruise-colored grackles arrived on the scene. Meager starlings. Rusty female cardinals. At each new mix, elated, they waited, but the loveliest of feathered winds never blew their way. And so the father taught him to love the ugly ones. Named them after earls and dukes, invested them with flight patterns to shame the baldest of eagles.

In the boy's front yard, truly, the meek had inherited the earth.

Such is the ornithology of family.

A boy flew away one morning to return a man to find his father turned to ash beside a bag of grainy seeds. And this note: Help me to fly.

Rejoice

Postcards, gas bills, love letters tinged with pheromones. I don't know whether it is an act of trust or a test of loyalty but people keep giving me things to mail. This is too much though. Marked undeliverable. Instead I will sit here dreaming of packages that open into a future they will never reveal. Only ritual, only more ritual: cats and dogs poised to hear bell chimes through a shifting maze of seasons. This nip in the air. Temple of June Bugs, Kingdom of Worms; the time of our awaited birth is awash in new currents, baptized in rivers of whiskey and winter. Strange flowers planted to pick or plow under. As you will.

Aleš Debeljak

Earth. Red earth. And tall grass as far as you can see. You're pressed to the ground. Hidden from unwanted glances. Utterly still. A quail by your ear. Are you turning into stone? No: you're just listening to shadows fall over cornfields. A bead of sweat—a tear?—slides down your cheek. In the distance a mountain rises steeply. Naked. Without trees or flowers. Imprinted on the sharp-edged horizon. On its peak, lost in the clouds, generations of stag hunters wander for centuries. Glistening of the setting sun. All the signs say end of Indian summer. If I hear it right, nothing comes from your lips. Are you dumb? Blind? Perhaps you're searching through memory for the shapes of all prints—footsteps in the snow, old songs and cognac in the evening, small white towns with castles and turrets, the smells of Sunday afternoons, the river running under granite bridges. As if this, too, escapes you. Here, under the empty sky of ancient tribes you never heard about, you'll end your way. I, of course, always return. You don't. Which makes all the difference.

Another beginning: it doesn't make any sense. I'd rather not even try again. And yet: this image, this faded photograph of you, your sad face, your hands on your lap (do I only imagine it?), in a room with friends—yet not altogether there. The photograph is still here. Along with all the things you wanted then. You know exactly what you believe! How carefully you choose your words, which sound so perfect! You talk today, whenever, with anyone. The children at your feet play with dominoes made from the bones of animals. Closets filled with smoked glass. Perhaps a book or two. Open on the shelf. Now you can tell me what you kept for years from the ones closest to you. The future's already here. Tell me everything. Ups and downs, the habits of your heart, silences, mild mornings, long-distance calls, sighs, whispers, hopes, fears. I'm no longer here for you to hurt. The gust of autumn wind in the chimes clinking on the balcony: only you can hear it.

Translated by Christopher Merrill.

STUART DYBEK

Alphabet Soup

In this place the soup was what one came for—alphabet soup for the Language poets—and a clear broth for everyone else. Here, ordering a steaming bowl of soup could be like visiting an oracle. Soup was a kind of lens: "a monocle for the mouth," in the unforgettable phrase of the renowned poet-dentist, Victor Guzman, D.D.S.

Despite its storefront appearance, it wasn't just another ethnic restaurant. It was too cosmopolitan for that. American poets of the International school table-hopped, suavely reciting their poems in what sounded like English translations. In those days, the so-called One-of-the-Boys-Gang of surrealists ate there, too. Do you remember them?

Adjacent to the restrooms, an old phone booth to which plywood siding had been hammered and a cross affixed, served as a makeshift confessional where the unrepentant Confessional poets lined up to dine, kneeling before their soup as if it could forgive them.

A table in a corner, way in the back, with only a single chair was where the Hermetics ate—one at a time.

The Academics frequented another place, just across the street, Bloom's Deli, where, to their clamorous orders, the bored Mrs. Bloom said nothing beyond *yes yes yes,* punctuated by an occasional *oy vey* as her customers deconstructed the brisket.

Ah! these allusions of grandeur!

At all the little tables, hunched over simmering controversies, various groups of poets slurped their soup. They had gathered like opposing, neighborhood softball teams gather at a neutral corner tavern after their games on Friday night in order to recount their exploits, to total and retotal the score, to study the rankings and their own particular statistics, to ascribe errors, dissect reputations, erect legends. Instead of Bud's Bombers or the Popes of Pilsen Park, they had names like the Formalist Strokers, the

Regionalist Whackers, the Multicultural Pounders, and the Dukes of Deep Image. The greasy light of soup illuminated their faces and made their eyes gleam. There were the Beats, sipping soup from a burbling hookah, the Political Poets memorializing the exploited between brimming mouthfuls, and the One-of-the-Girls-Gang of women poets, their spoons all clacking until invariably from some table or other someone would cry, "Garçon! There's a fly in my soup!"

A rare silence would befall the room, all eyes watching as the Garçon comes rushing to the table.

"There's a fly in my soup!"

"I see," the Garçon says. "Allow me," and he reaches into the bowl, unzips the soup's fly, and a penis, limp as a noodle, floats out.

"I say, what sort of soup have you served me? Take it away, take it to that empty window table reserved for the audience."

Russell Edson

Sleep

There was a man who didn't know how to sleep; nodding off every night into a drab, unprofessional sleep. Sleep that he'd grown so tired of sleeping.

He tried reading *The Manual of Sleep*, but it just put him to sleep. That same old sleep that he had grown so tired of sleeping . . .

He needed a sleeping master, who with a whip and a chair would discipline the night, and make him jump through hoops of gasolined fire. Someone who could make a tiger sit on a tiny pedestal and yawn . . .

Bread

I like good looking bread. Bread that's willing. The kind of bread that's found in dreams of hunger.

And so it was that I met such a bread. I had knocked on a door (I sometimes do that to keep my knuckles in shape), and a women of huge doughy proportions (she had that unbaked, unkneaded look) appeared holding a rather good-looking loaf of bread.

I took a bite and the loaf began to cry . . .

The Prose Poems as a Beautiful Animal

He had been writing a prose poem, and had succeeded in mating a giraffe with an elephant. Scientists from all over the world came to see the product: The body looked like an elephant's, but it had the neck of a giraffe with a small elephant's head and a short trunk that wiggled like a wet noodle.

You have created a beautiful new animal, said one of the scientists.

Do you really like it?

Like it? cried the scientist, *I adore it, and would love to have sex with it that I might create another beautiful animal . . .*

Jean Follain

You can get the impression that cities are really our point of contact with fate, spreading out their shimmering perspectives, the fans of their back streets. Hallways end at brown doors: behind them, you hardly hear the muffled sounds of couples. People don't always pass each other with blank faces. Sometimes their glances seem vulnerable. Often the public clocks are stopped: then time goes nowhere. But dawn, with its tranquil beauty, will bathe some monument's steeple or dome, or the first flowers in an indoor market where a freshly washed woman cries *Roses for Sale*.

A middle-aged man's wife tells him: "Put on your hat, you'll be cold." So he puts on his derby. It would take a long time to describe it, if you wanted to be exact: the band, the tight stitching at the brim that wears out faster than anything else, the white lining with the hat shop's name stamped in gold and rubbing off, the leather band inside with the wearer's monogram. During riots men wearing such hats were easy targets. They fell to the ground, their black hats rolling on the earth that was dry or cracked or sodden, or even covered with snow.

Alone at home now, the woman looks out the window, sees only a few trees and the sky.

Translated by Mary Feeney and William Matthews.

Val Gerstle

Mom Told Me to Grow Up
and Win the Nobel Prize

Mom told me to grow up and win the Nobel Prize. She taught me how to check my breasts for cancer and made sure I knew who Cezanne was. When I was sixteen, I put on cologne that smelled like chrysanthemums and let a pornographer take pictures of me sitting in icy water that made my nipples stick out like chimneys. On weekends he took me to the Parkette Drive-In. I saw *Kill and Be Killed* six times. The year I turned eighteen I got an apartment with a carpet, and took to wearing kneesocks and stickpins. A football player who became an insurance salesman after he tore the ligaments in his knee married me late that summer. The wedding was small, but I got a hotpad set, pink toilet cover, yogurt maker and flyzapper. My parents sent us to Sarasota for the honeymoon. A year later I was bored with diapers and daytime TV so I took a plane to California and changed my name and hair color! met a wiry young women who was doing research work with carrier pigeons. Since she was middle-class and I suddenly wasn't, she took me to lunch at a place with dark air and leather seats and stone jugs. We drank beer and she gave me a key to her apartment so I could have someplace decent to eat sandwiches and take showers and sleep. Then I went uptown and got a job as a typist in an ad agency. The Director liked me because I was young and didn't talk and typed fast. I was happy bringing home a paycheck each weekend. I made just enough to buy soap and sandwiches and a couple more tulip print dresses, and occasionally a luxury, like a bracelet for the scientist on her birthday. We put on our pajamas and sat in front of the TV and celebrated with crabmeat soup and gin straight from the bottle.

MAUREEN GIBBON

Un Bruit Qui Court

On the island, women are moored like boats.

In late summer the grass and ground vines of the island have dried. Crickets rub their wings together and all day long the brush on the side of the road ticks and scratches in the heat. Men have returned from the morning catch to sit at their dinners. Voices and the sound of knives and forks on plates come through the closed shutters of the island houses.

In the harbor the women wait. They are tied to logs sunken in the shore-bottom or to metal rings along the stone sea wall of the port. The paint on the boats is scorched, hot to the touch. It peels away in layers. These are small boats, skiffs, large enough for only one or two men. Fish swim beneath the boats in cool shadows.

The men do not understand that their women are moored boats. One side bakes and dries in the sun and the men know it is for carrying and ferry-ing, but the underside is a blue world they do not know how to see or har-vest. Sometimes a plank of wood splits in one of the boats because of the heat. The sound is sharp, like a handclap, but has a small cry or screech in it, too. And there is the plank, split in two. The men can do that with their heat, make a woman cry out. She may also split silently so that you would never know.

Blue Dress

I look like my mother when I wear the dress. I don't know why I say that
—there aren't any pictures of her in a cornflower blue dress with white
dots, and it isn't the kind of dress she wore. Just saying polka dots makes
me feel silly, but I feel beautiful and somehow womanly in the dress.

Maybe that's what it is: the dress makes me a woman I never thought I'd be,
older and flirtatious, someone who wears stockings and rouge, who sits a
long time at a kitchen table, drinking coffee and remembering. The dress
bares so much of me — the shy skin at my shoulders, the light hair of my
forearms, all the veins rising and crossing under the skin of my wrist. When
I wear the dress, I can imagine my arms wrapped around a man's shoulders,
my hands at the nape of his neck, my own waist tightly held. I think about
the words in my arms and can almost feel it, as if the words themselves were
touch, the way imagining brings feeling.

It's hard to explain what it means to see my own arms and hands change
after so many years of being young. I remember touching the backs of my
mother's hands when I was little. I thought they were cool beneath my fin-
gers, smoother than my sticky girl's hands. "No," my mother said. "Your
hands are softer. I used to nibble you when you were a baby, just to have
your skin in my mouth."

My hands are beginning to look like hers. The veins show easily and my
knuckles are starting to look bony. The skin doesn't give as much and seems
thin. I know it means I'm aging, but it comforts me. It's like wearing my
mother's old turquoise and pearl bracelet, or her engagement ring, reset with
a blue stone for my birthday. Sometimes when I think of my mother I won-
der how long she will live. My hands seem so small when I think of that.

GARY GILDNER

The Wolverine

Word got around town: a wolverine was being shown in Rae Brothers parking lot. Some last-minute Christmas shoppers went to look. Many of the younger people had never seen one before, not up close like this. It lay curled in the back of a pickup, on the tailgate, and someone—a small girl—said it looked like a big fuzzy caterpillar. The man holding her hand said, "See those teeth? You wouldn't want to fool with them!" And somebody else asked, "What is it?" The ranger, who had received it from the trapper, said it was a male. About thirty pounds. He said he was surprised: wolverines were supposed to have been long gone from the area. The trapper was surprised too: he'd been after bobcat. He had his foot up on a rear tire and was leaning against his knee; his hat was pushed back; he could look down and see the animal as he talked. The man holding the small girl's hand asked what he used to catch it. "A snare," the other said. "With that good aircraft cable that don't kink." He shook his head at the surprise of it all, or at the snare's effectiveness, or maybe only as a kind of punctuation; and a couple of older men, whose eyes were watery-bright from age, shook their heads too. It got cold standing there in Rae Brothers parking lot, and people began drifting away. One of these, a girl, said to her boyfriend, "I hate those things." He laughed, then flung his arm around her neck, pulling her closer.

Busy

I am busy living in the new millennium. It fits well with the depression I left back in the twentieth century. I am happier now because I am older and fewer birds fly after me. If I could grow a beard, I would. If I could take my time in deciding what I think of my country, it would be easier to live here without thinking I have to have an opinion, cast a vote, or drink distilled water. I am not sure where I am going with this, but it is a fine season for confessing how we made it past the zero hour. Even the tiny spider crossing the white rug in the living room is going to make it into the first decade of the new awareness. I don't step on it or call my cat's attention to it. The little spider passes the leg of the sofa and disappears. I read in the newspaper about the 20,000 fish that were found dead in the Guadalupe River near San Antonio. It turns out it was fire ant mating season. After male fire ants mate with the females in midair, they die. When wildlife people cut open the dead fish to see what killed them, they found thousands of fire ants in their bellies. The toxic poison of the male fire ants killed the fish after they gorged on the falling insects. I am busy thinking about this because I used to live in the area and was attacked by fire ants several times. This thought fits with what I was going to say. I have two large windows in my office and a large desk. When I open any book in my office, I always use both hands.

Miriam Goodman

Shopping Trip

I try on clothes with you and fifty other women in a mirrored room. Down to my pantyhose and bra, I step into a dress and hold my breath. The moment I know my body fails to fit, an apparition of my mother comes and warns me not to get involved with you. *You're fat and sad*, my mother says, wearing her half-size navy crepe, a window of lace at her breast. She also shopped for bargains.

I'm seeking our reflection in the mirrors, heavy, unsexual, trying a skin for the world. You look for slacks they can't see through. I look for skirts that hide me, yet push forward to be noticed. The stockgirls in the center of the room rehang the garments we discard like piles of novels taken back to shelve. I don't know how to dress the role you'd have me play: a woman who loves sex with women. It seems to me that I look bad in everything.

I ask if your grown daughters love you. "They'd better," you say, "since I don't love myself." We are alike in this as in less hidden things and yet we look for love to make us new. So let's get out of here and go pick up a turkey. We could slide our hands inside the carcass, roll them in the slippery juices, thinking of each other, of delight. "Look, there's the moon," I could tell you. And I could write you from the future: "Remember when?" I have nostalgia for this chance, and for my mother. And though I can't make love to you, I could make a turkey with her watching.

S. C. Hahn

Omaha

Dawn leaves a highway of blood running down the bluffs into the Missouri.

At the Union Pacific roundhouse, the doors roll open with a screech of metal, and great engines haul the heat of August out into the day.

A block away from St. Frances Cabrini church in Little Italy, the face of Christ grows on a Big Boy tomato in Mrs. Antonia Cabriatti's garden. She sits at her kitchen window, drinking coffee with cream and eating anisette toast, wondering whether to cook the tomato or report it to Father Vitelli. She would like to eat the face of Christ as a sauce on a nice fritatta, but she could never confess that to the priest.

Down Tenth Street at the Praha Bakery, Jim Kovar puts another ball of rye dough on his baker's paddle and places it into the brick oven. It is the same motion his grandfather used when he was an artilleryman in the army of Emperor Franz Josef. Whenever people eat Kovar's rye bread they bite into caraway seeds, and that little shell bursts into a cloud of remembering: the bread at the older Preshyl girl's wedding feast, the roast duck with skin goose-pimpled as boys skinny-dipping in an early May stream, steam rising from potato dumplings and kraut, tart Pilsener beer, the prune and apricot kolachy. Ah, memory is a fat midwife, they say, and the future is a thin bride.

Over on Thirteenth Street, Maria Kutzowski sells a Tootsie Roll to the Cantu kid, whose father Hector works in one of the packing plants. She remembers when this whole neighborhood was Polish and Lithuanian, but her children have all moved to the west side. At least these Mexicans are good Catholics, she thinks, not like all the apostate Lutheran Danes up around north 30th Street. She went up there once, she says in Polish to her friends over beers at the Vistula Tavern, and felt like she was in a foreign country. Not a kerchief to be seen on the heads of the women! But she would like to go again, because the men are handsome . . .

It is like that all over the rest of Omaha this morning: in the black community north of Dodge Street, where people are having breakfast and thinking about what they will do after work this evening; in the old Jewish neighborhood over by Central High; in the Serbian blocks by the foundry; in the dwellings of the Swedes and the Germans and the Irish and the Greeks, all the way west to Boys Town.

In every house, in every heart is a packing plant built of the slow-fired bricks of experience, where dreams hang on steel hooks in cold storage.

Marie Harris

Driving Lessons

Before our Town Dump became first a landfill then a waste transfer station, I'd back up to the edge of a smoldering mountain of garbage, let down the tailgate, climb into the bed, and fling trash bags, sheetrock scraps, dead appliances, broken rakes, used tar paper, tangled chicken wire, and anything else left over from our week's labor onto the pile. Smoke of a particular, unmistakable scent drifted in the air and beer bottles exploded like muffled firecrackers.

Neighbors lingered, exchanging gossip, keeping an eye out for anything that had no business being thrown away. Not infrequently, items brought to be discarded never hit the ground. Even I was not immune. I acquired a boy's bike this way—lacking only a pedal—a pair of waders in need of duct tape and a dusty pink bathroom scale.

Ray the dump keeper knew just about everyone in town, by sight if not by name. *Good morning, Mrs. Rockefeller,* he'd shout as I eased our rusting truck to a stop.

It was our only means of transportation in those days, the 1965 International pickup Charter had driven twice across the country and twice rebuilt the engine. I liked driving it despite having to double clutch on the downshift and haul on the steering wheel for all but the gentlest turns.

Charter loved that truck. He kept its oil changed and its innards lubed. He washed it regularly and in winter took care to spray water up under the wheel wells to remove road salt. One Christmas I had the bench seat reupholstered for him.

In the summer of his sixteenth year, Bill took the wheel. Charter sat to the right of the floormounted gearshift and they set off down the driveway. Within minutes the truck reappeared with a fresh dent in the left front fender. Bill took a slow turn at the mailboxes and kept on turning. Into the phone pole.

Anybody hurt?

Anybody hurt? was what my Dad used to say as each of his ten children in turn sent moving vehicles off embankments, into drifts, caroming into other cars and skidding into ditches.

On a snowy Good Friday, Sebastian passed his driving test in my old blue Pinto. The following summer he was rear-ended at a red light by a license-less, uninsured teenaged girl.

We both tried to teach Manny, but each lesson ended with him slumped over the steering wheel, defeated. Mr. Towle of Towle's Driving School had better success, though he did suggest that Manny take his course a second time. Mr. Towle wore a dark suit with a red tie. He drove a spiffy black Pontiac. Manny drove his spiffy black Pontiac. Down dirt roads and side roads and highways. For six weeks. (Mr. Towle is uncomfortable with failure. In his quiet way.) And on the roads for another six weeks. Manny passed the driving test. Mr. Towle is authorized to administer the written part of the test orally should he deem that necessary He did. Manny's license arrived in the mail.

The wet snow that fell last night is melting in patches. Manny drives slowly down the dirt road in the Chevy longbed we'd bought for him from a guy who owned a flooring business. He accelerates a little on the paved part. No weight in the back. Used tires. The truck begins to plane just as we reach the blind curve. When he swerves and hits the pine tree, my glasses fly off my face and Manny utters the one word he's never said in front of me.

Jim Harrison

My Leader

Now in the dog days of summer and Sirius making a dawn peek over the mountains, or so I think being fairly ignorant of stars. It's been over 90 degrees for thirty days and here in Montana the earth has begun to burn. I recall a hot late morning down in Veracruz in a poor folks cemetery waiting for a restaurant to open so I could eat my lunch, a roasted *roballo* with lime and garlic, a beer, a nap and then to start life over again watching ships in the harbor that needed to be watched. The old cemetery keeper points out a goat in the far corner and shrugs, making hand and finger gestures to explain how the goat crawls over the stone fence or wriggles though the loose gates. I follow the goat here and there and he maintains what he thinks is a safe distance. He eats fresh flowers and chews plastic flowers letting them dribble in bits from his lips. A stray dog trots down a path and the goat charges, his big balls swinging freely. The dog runs howling, squeezing through a gate. The goat looks at me as if to say, "See what I have done." Now he saunters and finds fresh browse in the shade of the catafalque of the Dominquez family. I sit down in the shade and he sits down facing me about ten feet away, his coat mangy and his eyes quite red. I say, "I'm waiting for my roasted fish." He stares, only understanding Spanish. I say, "In this graveyard together we share the fatal illness, time." He stretches for a mouthful of yellow flowers quickly spitting them out. Baptists say the world is only 4,000 years old but goats are fast learners. They know what's poisonous as they eat the world.

Very Small Wars

There's no flash here among the troops. We just want to protect our freedom, well being and safety. It occurred to me that if I were a vehicle I wouldn't be a Maserati but a John Deere or Farmall tractor, nothing that special. Way out here in the country Linda runs a trap line and I patrol daily for rattlers though I can't find the one she saw in the garage behind her gardening tools. She kills a half-dozen mice a day but is now thinking of a device called "Mice Cube" which merely traps them so I could release them on a Republican's lawn when I drive to town for a drink. I'm squeamish about killing mice once having tried to save one with a broken neck in the trap who looked up at me imploringly. I was drunk and actually sobbed, putting the little critter on a cotton bed in a matchbox. In the morning she was gone but was probably eaten by our retarded cat Elie who sits under the bird feeder all day waiting for lunch to fall from the heavens. Also there's a sentimentality about murder as I intend to shoot Hungarian partridge, grouse, woodcock, maybe an antelope for the table this fall. Linda is rather matter-of-fact about killing mice but women are natural hunters. Rattlesnakes aren't innocent. One killed my dog Rose. Our little grandson Silas walks in the flowerbeds which we pre-check for vipers. The mind tires of this war but my peace plan is faulty: let rattlers in the house to kill and eat the mice. The last rattler I shot was within a foot of the front door and struck at our old, deaf cat Warren. I blew the snake's head into oatmeal with my pistola in a surge of anger. I am a man of peace. Send suggestions. It's not known in Washington D.C. but death is death.

JENNIFER L. HOLLEY

The Rubbing

We both wake up in the night. On her way from the bathroom, she meets me in the kitchen, a glass of water in my hand. *Will you please rub my legs?* she asks. I take her arm, walk her back to bed. She stretches on top of the blanket, turns on her stomach, pulls off her turban, and spreads her fingers through the gray fuzz on her scalp. I lean over to stroke it, too, before dousing my hands in rubbing alcohol. I massage her calves until my hands burn from the heat between us. *All over,* she says. I move up the backs of her knees. Then up her thighs. She moans as if the pain worsens under my care. I notice the open door, and wish I had shut it. I find the creases higher on her legs and slide the sides of my palms in them, brushing along the lace hem of her nightgown. *Do you hurt all over?* I ask. *Yes,* she says, *even higher.* She quiets as I lift her nightgown and let it gather in the small of her back. She wears nothing else. I take her buttocks in my hands, knead them. I now know how soft and loose the skin of my own body will feel in thirty years. We have no words to travel through the walls, to wake up my sister so that she will walk in and see. Our mother, on her stomach, her gown hitched to her waist. Me, straddled over her body, about to collapse, on my knees.

BROOKE HORVATH

The *Encyclopaedia Britannica* Uses Down Syndrome to Define "Monster"

...humani nil a me alienum puto.
—Terence

I

The encyclopedia's definition leaves my daughter holding hands with Grendel, the Cyclops, Frankenstein's monster, the mythic deformities of hell.

Chancing upon this definition leaves me face to face with the unspeakable.

II

She is a monster who cries, recites with her sister the alphabet, has fallen in love with the boy at preschool who opens her yogurt for her.

She is a monster who meets with fear and stares outside and inside, holds the usual human emotions imprisoned by more than usual inarticulateness.

III

My insurance company will not pay for her therapy. Therapy, a letter tells me, is covered only following an accident.

My insurance company does not believe in genetic accidents. My insurance company covers only human beings.

IV

The *Encyclopaedia Britannica*, with its assurance that truth is tidy and know-able and humansized, can shove its learning up its human ass.

It is anything human that is alien to me.

V

My monster's favorite shirt has four hearts across its front. I ask her why she likes this shirt so much, and she points to the hearts.

You like hearts, I ask. But she shakes her head no, pointing again to each heart in turn and saying carefully: mommy, daddy, sister, me.

Ji-Woo Hwang

History

On December 29th, my mother threw steamed rice cakes into the sea in front of our house and smoothed its scattered waves. The next day a cold rain poured onto the laver field. We just looked into the eaves of the rainy spell: poverty was our custom. My heart at high tide worked harder, my cotton clothes carried the stench of my family's wet flesh. Hearing the current swiftly ebbing from the front yard, we remained at the lower shore.

The unnamed islands moved far from view, and the wooden boats that left late sailed back and forth between them. Instead of entering the sea, I listened to the sound of waves breaking over the jar stand in the back yard. In the empty jars the cries of the birds of Sol Island, from which my father left, never stopped. When I could no longer hear which valley deepened across the water, the receding southern bays cried bitterly.

My mother wouldn't let me go outside, and in the courtyard the smoke fluttered again. The myopic winter sea was thinning at the sparkling edge of my eyes. When my father was dragged from the house, the waves at the ferry were as calm as this. If I stood by the shore, flocks of exhausted water birds would be shoved into my dizzy knees. To me, they looked like white funeral flowers flown in from some remote island. The corollas of the flowers were so bright I wished I could fall asleep. In a flash I saw my father coming and going in my mother's dream of conception, and I crossed the oyster flats and hurled nets into the phosphorescent night sea. The flowers decorating my father's bier were endlessly crossing the early morning sea.

The wind that blows every two weeks raged. But the wind had no sound of the wind, like my body after death; the wooden ships returned empty. To avoid the smell of the seaweed, the birds flew from my knees to the interior. The people near shore followed the white cloth of their headbands and moved inland, while the women bowed two and three times for their reincarnation, throwing steamed rice cakes into the laver field in the rainy sea-

The Wooden Pony and My Daughter

The market's on the way home, and if you follow the lane for a hundred meters you'll find Honam Butcher's. If you take the lane by the fish shop on the right, you'll come to Silim Bath, a public bath. Behind the bath is an empty lot on which stand the salt shop and the tile factory. The salt shop is a wooden shack with a slate roof. Take the narrow path through the tenement houses. The eighth house, the half-slated one, is mine. I live in this house, translating books, writing articles, sometimes writing poetry. If my wife grows anxious, I take my five-year-old daughter to the empty lot and play with her. In the shadow of the tall sycamore old people play cards.

Some days an old man enters the shade, pulling a cart on which stand six wooden ponies. For 100 *won* a child can ride for 20 or 30 minutes. I put my excited daughter on the white pony, pulling its ear to rock it up and down. Ah, my pretty daughter looks as if she could break the springs of its four legs and fly into the sky before my eyes. Letting its mane wave in the wind, she seems to have entered into the sandy wind coming from the tile factory, into Noryung, the land in the Maritime Province of Siberia, or even into a distant invisible land.

Translated by Christopher Merrill and Won-chung Kim.

Holly Iglesias

Thursday Afternoon: Life is Sweet

I know what's happening, see what's coming, and try like mad to fight it. Tapioca simmers in the dented pot. *The Joy of Cooking* says to use a *bain-marie* but I say, *bain-marie, my ass.* That Rombauer woman never shopped at Goodwill a day in her life. (He'll be home in three hours.) I stir constantly, watch carefully because that's what the damned book says to do but any fool knows that the stuff is done when the spoon starts to drag.

Tapioca has many lives, grows a new skin each time a scoop's dug out. Those beady little eyes even though the cookbook insists on calling them pearls—bounce from the box all dry and nervous and then the hot milk leaches the starch out and makes a gluey mess. The book says, *Never boil the pudding,* but screw that: I love those thick, beige swells exploding like volcanoes, the sound as the surface breaks, the smell of burnt sugar at the bottom of the pot.

They tell you, *Spoon the pudding into individual cups,* but I put the whole mess in a plastic bowl and watch it quiver as it slides into the icebox. The kids like to press little dimples into it, then lick their fingers clean behind the icebox door so I won't know who did it. Me, I push clear through to the bottom of the bowl and my finger comes out so coated that it fills my mouth.

I leave the pot on the counter, won't wash it for hours. (Slob, he'll say, but I'm learning to ignore him.) The residue dries into a sheet as sheer as dragonfly wings and the kids will peel it off, laughing and drooling as it melts in their mouths. I can hear them yell now as they race up the driveway, pitch their bikes against the gate. The screen door slams and in rushes the smell of them: sweat, cotton, soap, candy.

David Ignatow

A Modern Fable

Once upon a time a man stole a wolf from among its pack and said to the wolf, "Stop, you're snapping at my fingers," and the wolf replied, "I'm hungry. What have you got to eat?" And the man replied, "Chopped liver and sour cream." The wolf said, "I'll take sour cream. I remember having it once before at Aunt Millie's. May I bare my teeth in pleasure?" And the man replied, "Of course, if you'll come along quietly," and the wolf asked, "What do you think I am? Just because I like sour cream you expect me to change character?" The man thought about this. After all, what was he doing, stealing a wolf from its kind, as if he were innocent of wrongdoing? And he let the wolf go but later was sorry; he missed talking to the wolf and went in search of it, but the pack kept running away each time he came close. He kept chasing and the pack kept running away. It was a kind of relationship.

Without Recrimination

It is wonderful to die amidst the pleasures I have known and so to die without recrimination towards myself and others, free of guilt at my shortcomings, happy to have lived and happy to know death, the last of living, my spirit free to sing as when I felt it born in my youth. The youth of it returns in dying, moving off from anger that racked its throat.

With death before me, I look back at my pleasures and they were you whom I held close in loving, and in the poems I've written for this truth, which is their beauty and lets me die in pleasure with myself. I did not fail my life.

MAX JACOB

Mystery of the Sky

Coming back from the ball, I sat down at the window and gazed at the sky: it seemed to me the clouds were the huge heads of old men sitting at a table and someone brought them a white bird all decked out. A big river crossed the sky. One of the old men looked down at me, he was even going to speak when the spell was broken, leaving the pure twinkling stars.

Pre-War

What crowds on Sunday evenings for those dinner-dances at the Colonnes!
Look at the two drinkers getting up to dance. The bright hat of the accomplice is a pair of wings, and the lady vanishes with the rustling of a dove.
Poor dear, am I supposed to pity you? The face of the dancer labels what
he is, and the shadows between columns tell you where, through the smoky,
ruined tables, he is leading you.

Reconstruction

All it takes is a five-year-old in pale blue coveralls drawing in a coloring book for a door to open into the light, for the house to be built again and the ochre hillside covered with flowers.

Translated by William T. Kulik.

SIBYL JAMES

Le Nouveau Temps

The water's cut off again tonight. They must be digging on the new highway, working around the clock to paint white arrows, connect street lamps, at least on the strip between here and the presidential palace, so Ben Ali's black cop-flanked limousine can cut red ribbons on the new route on November 7th, the anniversary of the coup, the date of what the party calls *le nouveau temps,* the new time. They like to ring that date in with such ribbons, the paint on the latest metro stop or highway cloverleaf still dripping. Only the dark vans of police make continuity on every corner, the new time in the same old story. The stones in the graveyards head toward Mecca. On the roofs, the satellite dishes aim the other way.

LOUIS JENKINS

Tamaracks

In the evening I am drawn to the tamaracks that bend and straighten in the wind like oarsmen pulling the long boat. It is only the longing to be safely dead, the desire for peace. But perhaps, even in death you would be restless, driving the back roads, a pocket full of change for the telephone, calling across the country at a terrible hour. I think that ghosts are the insomniacs among the dead. The only dead man I ever talked to told me that there used to be a tennis court where my house is now. "That's right. I used to walk here in the evenings when I was a young man." I was impatient. I said, "I want to hear what things are like for you now." He said, "Oh people always ask me that. Can you explain to a child what it's like to be grown up. It's the same thing. I can tell you this though, times change. I was a blacksmith but I had to get into small engine repair in order to stay in business." "Oh, crap!" I said, and he vanished. The tamaracks accept the darkness just as the little pools of water accept the last portion of light. The air takes the water, leaving the road clear and dry.

JUAN RAMÓN JIMÉNEZ

Dreaming on the Train . . . No, in My Berth

The night was a long, firm black pier. The sea was the dream and led to eternal life. Along the coasts we were leaving—immense undulating moon-lit prairies—the crowds of the world, dressed in white and sleepy, waved goodbye to us with an immense emotion-filled clamor. Yes, yes. Hurrah for the winning horse! And white kerchiefs waving (New London), and straw hats, and green, purple and cinnamon parasol. . . .

I was standing in the prow—from up there one can see divinely well!—that ascended sharply to the stars and plunged deep into the bottom of the shadow—fine black horse!—tightly embracing . . . whom? No . . . no one . . . . But . . . there was someone waiting at the station for me who embraced me laughing, laughing, springtime woman. . . .

On the Shores of Sleep

Every night before going to sleep, I fill the riverbanks of my imagination with pleasurable qualities taken from the best of reality, so that its channeled dream reflects, intertwines, and carries them to infinity, like flowing water. Yes, how eager I am to not spill into the dawn any of the grim squalid nightmarish waters of this commercial city, of 8th Avenue, Chinatown, the El or the subway; I yearn to cleanse, like a pure wind from some other place, its smoky dry carmine, with the brilliant transparency of a pure, free, strong heart! How I long to smile in dreams, to move joyfully along these black stretches of night's dark road interrupted by patches of light, of day, towards death—brief glimpses of it; to see life as blue, rose and white, not under the light and power of consciousness, but to travel through a diamond mine, slowly, rather than to speed in a train, through this underground of night!

Translated by Mary Berg and Dennis Maloney.

Jim Johnson

The Things a Man Keeps

The things a man now keeps in the cab of a pickup truck: friction tape, jumper cables, county map, dinosaur bones, pliers, coffee mug with Town Pump logo, so many legal papers, letters to be mailed, maybe a tumbleweed or two, and, as we sharply turned the corner by the fairgrounds, a box, a small sealed cardboard box that slid along the dashboard all the way to the edge, struck the windshield, and fell to my feet. *That's my dad*, he said.

Peter Johnson

Pretty Happy!

I have no siblings who've killed themselves, a few breakdowns here and there, my son sometimes talking back to me, but, in general, I'm pretty happy. And if the basement leaks, and fuses fart out when the coffee machine comes on, and if the pastor beats us up with the same old parables, and raccoons overturn the garbage cans and ham it up at 2 o'clock in the morning while some punk is cutting the wires on my car stereo, I can still say, I'm pretty happy.

Pretty happy! Pretty happy! I whisper to my wife at midnight, waking to another night noise, reaching for the baseball bat I keep hidden under our bed.

Return

End of the twentieth century and I'm still angry. The new hero same as the old hero. And the poets? They're out back wrestling in the wet mulch, writing each other love letters with bird shit on brown paper bags. Just want to don my pajamas and curl up with a good book, but there aren't any. "Take it easy, Lady Philosophy," you warn. "Whoa there, Mr. Negativity." You're pointing to your souvenirs: jodhpurs from Jodhpur, an artificial ass from the court of Louis XIV, an eyelash of Catherine the Great. I shave my head, put on my swim cap limed with Bengay. I sit in a corner, sifting through the ashes of famous people. It's a metaphor, gentle reader. It's not a metaphor, gentle reader. Like everyone else, we wanted to become a legend, or a footnote to an obscure anecdote. We were driven by the certainty of heavy soil and that starlet's buttocks. And I wanted to Educate you, and would have, if the cockroaches hadn't eaten our canoe. There was certainly no ostriching on my part; I faced down every truth, every falsehood. "On my trip I met a woman named DNA," you croon, with that silly look on your face, then ask to play outside with the Famous Poet, who's holding a sacred fish over his head, saying, "When the hook is caught in the lower jaw that means your *vahine* has been unfaithful." This is not a metaphor, gentle reader. Not even a Strange Fact of the Week. Just a little jab to keep us moving, to keep us on the run.

Maurice Kenny

1911

Those fields and orchards. Barns hot with swallow flight. Your father's yellow rosebush circling the drive to the old homestead leaning into greyness, yet standing sturdy in the laughter of seven young girls ginghamed to the throat, swollen in wool though June, stepping sprightly across fields and into berries brightening meadows under larks and thrushes, pheasants fanning brush through woods of day lilies late to spring early to summer while your mama stood on the long front porch rotting beneath her feet screaming to the afternoon as her hands rose from wrinkled apron to hair whisking about her oval face shrouded in spots of anger that her seven daughters played on the neighbor's lawn.

The apple tree, translucent, yellowing the hour, ridiculous in its spiney, wobbly erection, tended with fervent hands by "pa," arching in birth of leaf and blossom, scenting the heavy air as wisteria weights the breeze; the apple for teeth, for sauce, for jack, for pie; the apple, symbol to your "pa" what has been and can be in its aging bend with no new branches struggling through winter snows to break open spring. Disappointment that young Charles died a babe. The apple, shade to chickens and gobblers; the apple where your mama threw out the coffee grinds, cabbage leaves, egg shells, wet corn cobs.

We loved it. Your grandma, my grandpa, you, us. (Four years ago, the house depleted in a hunter's ruin, old boards nailless from greed, old walls stripped of paper, not even a dented bedpot left in the rubble. The house down about the heads of the ghosts, crumbled into the spring cellar where brine once kept pork and pickles, where carrots and squash stayed bright and crisp. And all the voices, the voices of birth, and the wails of death, and the joy of holiday...came tumbling down.)

Oh! Mama, there was seldom happiness there. But beauty stood its ground. The earth shuddered, the fields, the orchards now bitter to the touch and the taste, the chicory, the bats of evening, the pitchers of ginger beer, iced melon. No, there was never happiness there while your "pa" spent his winter nights reading from the Bible in the barn, his place, allocated by your mama who would never allow his pipe in the parlor, your dirty stockings on the bedroom floor. Girls were raised to work, carry water for the laundry, wash dishes, scrub floors, shake the tick in the morning wind, scythe the grasses, and bend, bend, forever bend in the berry fields where you bled profusely on the fruit. Your face and gingham spotted with your first knowledge, your first lesson. You were never able to wash the blood away. It stuck, hard and dark to your cheek, your hands. And you cried in the fields where iris brightened the morning still heavy with dew and night-fear, where hawks gleaned the grain of mice and woodchucks, where the mirage of old women, hideous in masks, came to pinch your arm and whisper terrible tales into your ear. Beware of the night, the shade and the wind that comes out of the west. Beware of the breath. Let me touch your hair. And it turned white. You were a child and your hair turned white at the washer wringer. You screamed and the hideous old woman laughed a cackle that frightened the cocks crowing to the hens. And your mama spanked and took away the dessert from supper, a dish of gooseberry sauce. You wept in bed from all sorts of pain. Pain that would never leave your breast, your breast little and as pretty as a flower bud, a little fist that would open to mouths you never really learned to comprehend.

And the blood stayed on your cheek. It was there last month in the coffin. Brilliant in its birthmark. Not even my kiss washed it away. But the fields remain though barren without cow, a blind horse, a child's print. The fields, the land reeking with ghosts and voices gurgling the temper of the times. Deplete. Fields returning to scrub woods. And so it should be.

1982

Home. To fields and woods. To the frightening river I shied and the hills my horse cropped early June mornings. The fence that tore my calf when Lightning panicked and took me over the fence and cliff. The scar remains indelibly creased on the flesh. It is for this reason I remember, and I remember nearly everything.

I etch on the walls of my study. Hawk's feathers, a swallow's nest, sweetgrass, pebbles, and old boards collect dust blown off each time the imaginary tick sucks blood from behind my ear. I carry out yellowed snapshots. Grandpa leading his white horse to the trough. You big with Mary, Agnes in your arms...myself not the twinkle of your wildest thought, or fear. You loved photographs. Your walls crawled with them...Martin, in War Uniform proudly riding a tank, Pat in his Marine blues; Mary young and beautiful her eyes flashing. Agnes dressed in her Catholic Uniform from the Conservatory. Myself, a snip of adolescent confidence. A known lie. Façade. They were all façades. And you believed in them. It was all you had to believe. Photos that left old dust marks on the walls when he took them down and threw your dreams into the garbage. You sat night after night with the album by your side on the couch usually with your arthritic hand touching your babies, what you thought were your loved ones. (Do you know my father secretly carried your snap in his pocket until he died.) Is life merely a photograph? For some. For you.

He let you die alone. He told no one. Deprived. Depleted like your old homestead. The hunter took the kill and left you a crumble of old bones like boards, broken windowpanes. You went into death without a yellow rose from your father's circle. Denied. Your spirit as thin and transparent as saran. You hated cold. And you were freezing. February. And all your hopes lay in tubes and vials. I can see you spitting up your hospital supper. I can hear you say, I must lose weight, though you weighed barely eighty pounds.

Eighty pounds of disappointment and hurt. He allowed you to die alone. The man you feigned adoration for, the man whose puke soiled your age, whose vomit of cheap sweet wine you bent and cleaned. Oh! Mama! He didn't love you. He didn't even like your cooking. You became a drag on his cane. You were his cane and his hammer and his claw. You became everything despicable to him. Until now. Now that you are a part of the root of that cedar on your father's grave next to you. Now he remembers how beautiful your face had been and how straight your back, and firm your breast, how sweet your mouth. Now he touches reality. His right foot is about to step into shadow. You are revenged. Not that you probably want to be. But I want you to be revenged...for everything. Even my own father who was as cruel as his love could be, as any love, as all love can be. Even though he carried your snapshot into the rattle of his death.

We're still reaching for an understanding. Of so many things.

You stayed a girl. Withered age was merely a mask. Your flirt was always on the fingertip as it pressed a hand, or placed a wedge of pie before a guest. You lived crossing the bridge into Canada. You never really learned you can't cross into lands where you aren't wanted. (Nor have I, really.) You never got the lice completely out of your hair. You couldn't cut cords of any kind. You never buried the placentas. Like a boy you played mumblety-peg and lost each time you played. What was your final happiness? Your father's grave. To know Ruth and Jennie were there watching the men shovel earth. Your sisters admitted to loving you.

Mary A. Koncel

The Big Deep Voice of God

That morning Tommy Rodriguez heard a voice, so he piled his family into the car and headed down the interstate. "Take off your clothes," he ordered after a while. And because Tommy had heard the voice, maybe the big, deep voice of God, they all obeyed, watched shirts and underpants fly out the window, twisting and turning like strange desert birds.

Around noon, Tommy's wife began to wonder. She hadn't heard the voice but thought if she did it would call her "Sugar." "Sugar," it would say, "your thighs are hives of honey, and I am the Bumblebee of Love." Quivering slightly, she pressed her left cheek against warm blue vinyl.

At home she often wondered too. There, on those late summer evenings, she leaned across the sink into still white clouds of steam and listened. Opening her mouth, she always took in more than air and water.

Tommy drove a little faster, beyond the vast and restless sand, a failing sunset, the tangled fists of tumbleweed. In the backseat, Grandpa whined, and Aunt Maria began to pee. Tommy closed his eyes. He was sure salvation was just one billboard or gas pump away, sure the voice was whispering now. "Drive like the wind," it was telling him, "like a wild saint in the Texan wind."

After the Weather

Yesterday a man was sucked out of an airplane over the blue tipped mountains of Bolivia. He didn't cry "Emergency." He didn't buzz the stewardess. He just dropped his fork, opened his mouth, and let the wind gather him inch by inch.

The other passengers agreed. This was real life, better than the movie or chicken salad. They leaned out of their seats, envying the man, arms and legs spread like a sheet, discovering raw air and the breath of migrating angels.

Below, an old peasant woman beat her tortilla. She never dreamed that above her a man was losing his heart. Perhaps she was a barren woman and, when he landed, she'd say, "Yes, this is my son, a little old and a little late, but still my son."

And the man, he thought of wind and flocks of severed wings, then closed his eyes and arched himself again. He didn't understand. His head began to ache. He understood Buicks, red hair, the smell of day old beer. But not these clouds, this new, white sunlight, or the fate of a man from Sandusky, Ohio.

Kim Kwang-Kyu

Spirit Mountain

In my childhood village home there was a mysterious mountain. It was called Spirit Mountain. No one had ever climbed it.

By day, Spirit Mountain could not be seen.

With thick mist shrouding its lower half and clouds that covered what rose above, we could only guess dimly where it lay.

By night, too, Spirit Mountain could not be seen clearly.
In the moonlight and starlight of bright cloudless nights its dark form might be glimpsed, yet it was impossible to tell its shape or its height.

One day recently, seized with a sudden longing to see Spirit Mountain—it had never left my heart—I took an express bus back to my home village. Oddly enough, Spirit Mountain had utterly vanished and the unfamiliar village folk I questioned swore that there was no such mountain there.

Pagoda Tree

The local people used to call that tree where every night the owl came and shrieked a pagoda tree.

The pagoda tree cast a broad shadow by the well side. The bucket vanished, a pump appeared; later they introduced a piped water supply, and in that place a short while ago a filling station arose, but still the pagoda tree stands there unchanged.

During the Korean War, the bombed-out wreck of an army truck lay for a long time abandoned beneath the pagoda tree. After any items fit for the scrap dealers had been torn away, it became a plaything for the children and for almost 3 years that great lump of iron lay there rusting red until at last it broke up and disappeared.

A few scraps of shrapnel stuck into the pagoda tree too, but those bits of metal gradually rusted and were absorbed by the sap; finally a gnarl appeared over the spot. At some time or other a nature protection sign was hung there.

When I look at that pagoda tree, still now I long to stroke its great bulk, to lean against it, go climbing up into it, even to become its roots or branches. And whether I'm hurrying along on foot, or in a taxi, whenever I pass before it a feeling of shame arises.

For I keep thinking that motion is what that pagoda tree is doing, while standing fixed in one spot today as of old is what in reality I myself am doing.

Translated by Brother Anthony of Taize.

Nancy Lagomarsino

Worries about Mother and Dad pursue me through a crowd of golden-rod and into pinewoods, where the sound of the brook relaxes my eyes, allowing me to gaze outward. I come here often, seeking the silence water imposes when it takes on a voice. Across the ravine, lichen-covered boulders hold themselves still, as though departing glaciers told them to wait. It feels strange to be so involved with my parents again, after decades of comfortable distance.

When I woke from the dream that is childhood and went into the world, I carried the dream with me—you might say I've treated my childhood like a favorite shirt worn every day. How could I leave my childhood in a drawer? For so long, it was my only garment. Photographs show me gliding along with my family, but inwardly I was reliving one of those vivid dreams we remember more easily than the day and night that surround it. Today, I balance on a stone that rises above the brook, close to my parents, yet removed. Caught in the current, a small branch hurtles past like a child on a bicycle.

October leaves are falling, and Dad rakes one part of the front lawn over and over. Two years ago this month, our old dog Max died of cancer. The grayer his muzzle, the more I treasured him. He was put to sleep in his own bed, head erect, radiating dignity as the needle entered his leg. When his neck relaxed, David caught his head.

The day before, I'd been seized with grave-digging fever. I chose a protected spot on the edge of the back lawn, visible from the kitchen window. Following the vet's instructions, I dug down three feet, measuring with my yardstick, clipping roots, carving perfect corners in the clay. Next morning, I lined the bottom with pine needles. The rain held off. After the vet had driven away, we wrapped Max in a white sheet, carried him to his grave, and lowered him while he was still warm. We were careful with his tail. We put in his water dish, his collar and his toys, shoveled in a thick blanket of dirt, and laid a piece of slate on top. Later, when it started to rain, I rushed out with a tarp.

This was a dog I'd sometimes treated roughly, impatiently, a terrier mix of unknown lineage I'd walked with, caressed, and complained about for nearly fifteen years. We gave one another an understandable life. I was proud of his body, his feet and penis rather big for a thirty-five-pound dog, his bedroom eyes, his chin whiskers that hid pills, his tail that wagged in circles instead of back and forth. He could be a black and white blur, or as slow as a local train. I held his face in my hands, kissed his nose, and said good-bye. For so long, I looked into the future to study his death. Now, still unprepared, I must look into the past.

The paths Max wore away in his years of guarding us are grown over, though I keep thinking I see him limping toward me. The lawn raked bare will grow again. The leaves will accumulate, and no one will try to remove every single one. The days will drift down, the day my father dies among them, a fragile veil similar to the others, as if all from the same tree.

JAY LEEMING

Law Office

I am sitting in an adjustable chair on the 32nd floor of a skyscraper in New York City. I am typing a list of a thousand names into a computer. As I work I am listening through headphones to a recording of the journals of Cabeza de Vaca, a Spanish explorer who traveled to the United States in the 15th century. The office is air-conditioned and I am wearing a tie. A hurricane has drowned half of de Vaca's crew, and most of the rest are sick and dying of starvation on an island off the Florida Keys. The names I am entering are plaintiffs in a case against Union Carbide chemical company, and about half of them are deceased. Some filing cabinets are behind me; one is marked "Bhopal" and another reads "Breast Implants." The secretary sitting beside me goes to get a cup of coffee. De Vaca and his crew have eaten their horses, and are now sailing in a makeshift raft that uses their hides for sails. I keep typing. At noon a man comes through the office and waters all the plants. Every hour another sailor dies of pneumonia, or loses his grip and slides off the raft into the storm.

LARRY LEVIS

The Leopard's Mouth Is Dry and Cold Inside

Now I am drying my body, but carefully, as if it doesn't really belong to me, and won't last. And now that I see it, alone like this in the mirror, I think I'm right; it won't last. After all, does a stray dog feel permanent when you touch it? Does something as singular as this ant on my sill? Or if I admit that stray dogs and ants might have a certain anonymous permanence, why doesn't my white, bruised skin? It doesn't look as durable as my wife's reading glasses. It doesn't even look as if it will outlast some clouds I once saw. They were cramped into the sky of a child's painting, and looked as if the child forgot to include them, and then suddenly remembered and put in too many of them, as if to make sure of something.

P. H. LIOTTA

In Melville's Room

His smile tells us that he thinks we're idiots. *It's our honeymoon* I say. *My parents sent us.* He calls his daughter from the back to mind the store and takes us up the creaking stairs to floors of tilting oak. A room: cramped as the berth of a ship, and a couch of interlocking antlers beneath a window which overlooks the dead Nantucket winter. We browse among the books, the odds and ends. Not much remains. But here the man became his words: the wreck of *The Essex* and the whale, the vision that trails beneath all mortal acts, what little there is to live on when the spirit of a place has died. *Seen enough?* We lie, tell him that we have.

GIAN LOMBARDO

On the Bias

I know a man who thinks a perfect day is one that's wasted. No, not that one is *wasted*—I wouldn't dare say such a thing—but one in which nothing is accomplished whatsoever.

No events. No one pile (no matter how great or small) moved from one place to another.

It would have to be a perfect cipher with no exclamation of some beautiful thing or with no adrenalin rushing through your veins in response to some horrific threat.

Not even a morality play, without the tiniest degree of allegory, without a cat that might represent something else (say, the kitchen door or the roof or the third person in a *ménage à trois*) in the grasp of an owl that may be a sign of something else, but not—certainly not—of any reflection of boredom with its hunger.

KATHLEEN MCGOOKEY

Simple Arithmetic

I am still imagining the men lined up, the ones I imagine who want me. I'll tell you everything I know: there was a boy, a girl, and a boat. And palm trees, but the mosquitoes on the island chased them back to the boat. There was a boy, a girl, and a dog: I still can't get the story straight—magic fruit? straw into gold?—and night's black velvet has arrived. I am glad for my life and the high clear voices of four-year-olds in the Allegan Public Library. I am not the girl in the story—I am the girl whose mouth is mainly shut but who imagines it open. But where are the other boy and girl? Holding hands and walking into the library while a baby falls out of a pile of money with astonishing grace. She's afraid to go beyond the normal bounds of conversation, the simple arithmetic of the heart. An electric blue butterfly darts in front of the car, just beyond reach and the camera's focus. The clocks tick, their greedy faces shine. The money will always fall out of our hands. We will always be slightly out of place, standing behind ourselves, not getting anywhere—no island, no boat, and no one to save us.

A Fine Evening

It was a fine evening, we'd say later, a fine evening followed by an even finer morning: a misty sunrise stained the sky pinker by degrees. Light fell on the blue thistle and did not change its nature. A mole followed his star-shaped nose underground, in his private inky sky. Time has never stopped just for me. When the fog lifted, we saw the dew like jewels all over the lawn. Then multiple veils, multiple jewels, and grandmother's ribbon of thought was privately unlaced. We had planned a romp in the park, but she kept saying, "You're on a long vacation; you're certainly far from home," when really she was far from home. Her daughter kept trying to straighten things out. Well, why not try to improve things, even a little? She said she had nothing to wear to the picnic, even after we said her suitcase was in the car. In the park, high winds had blown the sunflowers' pale petals away: the bare centers were stark on the stalks, and the stalks had fallen over. The crows in the trees would not stop their rustling, their raucous whispers. When grandmother sat on the blanket, she said, "Do not help me, I am full of tears." We had argued about what kind of candy she'd like. I'd let my morning glories die because I didn't think the weather, such good weather, would last into October.

CHONGGI MAH

Case Report VI

—for little Anne Sanders

Until I became the father of a child, a patient was just a patient, old or child alike; until I became a father, I treated them like a machine, responding with unseen fury to their tears; until I became the father of a pretty child growing day by day, a flower of empathy never once came budding in my eyes.

After a thick needle had been inserted into your breastbone and you had been diagnosed with a disease that left you not long to live, I avoided your sickroom; when you waved your hand with feverish cheeks I once again became a bewildered wanderer. Then on the day when you were dying in my arms, I gazed at you, so pretty in life. Ah, now I'm budding with pain; your pain has become a sound of water that whispers night and day.

Don't resent, child. Don't resent that mob of philosophers who claim that once someone dies anywhere in the world, that's the end of it. You are kinder than they are. The older someone grows, the greater the amnesia, it seems, and eyes that see only what is visible grow dim. They are laughing, child, but after you died you showed me clearly—alive or dead, there is no parting.

Sesame Flowers

Sesame seeds, that lived separate lives as they slept buried in the ground, produce fragrant sesame leaves, bloom with the lovely little white sesame flowers that will one day blossom as a milky mist amidst a host of sesame leaves, and you, soil, produce moist sesame seeds before even all the sesame flowers have been seen. What bargain have you made with the sesame seeds that you provide them with such solid, abundant bodies?

Likewise, how do all the flower-seeds I cannot see clearly with my weakening eyesight produce the fragile, delicate skin of the red and purple flowers I can see so clearly in this back garden? Where are the earth's dye factories, needlework factories, perfume factories, that enable this little flower to blossom and laugh here, its white dress girt thinly about with a pink belt?

Is it because my common sense is growing more and more vague with age that the things people incline to think normal seem to me increasingly abnormal? At least tell me, land of mystery rising on my ever vaguer common sense, if we are ever able to draw close to you, will we recognize your prudent skill? Or at least will we be able to watch and enjoy every day your charming magic as earth becomes flowers, earth becomes sesame seed?

Eye-openings of knowledge like sesame seeds, as my growing curiosity gradually finds answers; today once again I sit beside a sesame flower and wait for a flickering word, and on that day when my flesh becomes a sesame flower will you be able to recognize that my words and writing have at least been able to emit fragrance? Will you be able to recognize that the days when I wandered in search of the song I wished to sing have turned into fresh life at last?

Translated by Brother Anthony of Taize.

DENNIS MALONEY

Who Are the Heroes

Mid-November.

I walk through the square, across the grass tinged white. A dusting of snow settles on the gold and crimson leaves. They will be pressed to the ground beneath the sodden weight all winter till they become transparent nets of veins giving what little they hold back to the earth.

In the center of the square stands the statue of a now forgotten Civil War general, mounted on horse prepared to charge into battle. Across the stone pedestal someone has scrawled with black paint "The peace makers are the heroes."

Here the general sits, eyes alert, spurs digging into the flanks of his horse. He carries a sword raised above his head, leading the charge, plunging into battle. Into the shouts and cries, the gunsmoke, and blood. What was that last thought as the bullet pierced your flesh?

The boy of twelve or fourteen receives a gun from his father and gives up playing. He walks down a country road alone, gun slung over his shoulder. A gold finger ring lost for centuries is found among the ruins. On it the goddess stands at a small shrine, bare breasted, between two men; one is tearing out a tree by the roots, the other kneels weeping.

A Place Not Easily Filled

I remember my first visit to this supermarket after moving into the neighborhood. I was still hung over from too many farewell rounds the night before. Even hung over I marveled at the wood floors. Wood floors I thought! When was the last time I'd seen wood floors in a supermarket? Floors of character, varnish worn off, with scrapes and scars showing the years.

Buying a few necessities, I returned to the pile of cartons and furniture that would gradually begin to resemble a home.

I didn't know you well, only one among the several who checked out my groceries and with whom I exchanged coin and pleasantry. You became visibly pregnant along with the coming spring and with the slow arrival of summer, took leave to give birth. I never gave a thought as to your return. But one day you were suddenly there at the register ringing up soap and beer, making change, as before.

Not long after, returning from a weekend out of town, I stopped by the store to pick up some groceries and found it strangely closed. The TV news that evening held the answer. Two young men had entered the store that morning bent on robbery and made their way to the office demanding money with the revolver drawn. You gave them all there was, yet they let a bullet fly as they fled. It pierced your body, your young body which had so recently blossomed.

The words of your death exploded in my stomach as if the bullet had ripped through me. It was a week before I could enter the store, filled with a hollowness, a place not easily filled.

Morton Marcus

The Request

Suddenly Bjorling's voice on the stereo: "As a request, I should like to sing for you Schubert's 'Serenade.'" The crowd applauds and with a cascade of piano music framing the lyrics, he sings.

But my tears had started—hot, unexpected—at hearing his words, for I was aware that the man making this announcement on the stage of Carnegie Hall in 1958, his voice clipped and formal with a foreign intonation, would be dead within two years.

Who made the request and what motivated it? A shared melody with a loved one in a long ago Vienna or Shanghai? The memory of an age moldering behind closed doors, where the faces of baroque cherubs and the tiles of upswept Chinese roofs were cracked and broken long before they were the wreckage of cities under siege?—long before millions of arms and legs twitched in mass graves? Or maybe not that. Maybe the singer—thick-chested, square-faced—having witnessed wars and depredations, was requesting permission to sing one more song for everything that was gone. Whatever the reason, after the applause and encased in the piano's melody, the voice streaked through the hall, entered the recording apparatus, and now cleaves the heated air in my living room years later, rolling back the present on two sides to make way for its arrival from the past, like a deluge of sunlight tumbling through an opening in the clouds to the valley below, letting us glimpse for a moment a possibility of redemption in a tumult of wings.

But what's this!—the voice unexpectedly summons up the image of my father in the photograph I'd long forgotten: he poses from the waist up in a business suit, his right arm extended, as if delivering an aria, and I realize that he looked enough like this tenor I've idolized for years to be his brother—the same stocky build and beefy features—and the words I'm hearing now are coming not from the tenor's lips but from my father's half-remembered face, that face I'd seen only twice, and then for barely several minutes, and whose only words I can remember, "So, you're my son," expressed neither approval nor disapproval, just an affirmation that I existed—a statement made not for me but for himself.

But now, Father, your voice is so clear. Sing to me the old songs of love and loss and continuing on. Let your voice soothe me, an old man myself now, older than you ever were, but more in need of a lullaby on this battered earth than I ever was as a child. Sing from the past about what seems irrevocably gone but always returns, so once again I can believe in the guiding presence of fathers and the healing power of song.

Jussi Bjorling, the great tenor with the Metropolitan Opera in the 1940s & '50s.

The Moment for Which There Is No Name

On the sixteenth floor of one of the tall old buildings in the north end of the city, the windows of an apartment look out over the bay. The apartment is empty, the floors and walls bare. There is only a chalked circle on the living room floor. The circle traces the spot where an armchair once stood, an armchair in which an old man regularly sat watching the smokestacks come and go in the harbor in the same way he had watched the swaying forests of masts when he was a boy, years before he became a bookkeeper for one of the city's three tool and die works.

The circle was drawn by the old man's grandson while the child's parents were supervising the movers.

Tomorrow the new tenants will arrive, and preparatory to moving in they will clean the apartment. In the course of their cleaning, they will erase the chalk.

That is the moment for which there is no name.

Peter Markus

Black Light

For years he had heard his father talk about work, about carbon boils, tap holes, skulls of frozen steel. And he had spent many nights lying in bed awake, nights his father worked the graveyard shift, wondering what it all meant, as if the mill, and the life that went on inside it, was a part of some other world: a world he and his mother did not belong to. But one day all of this changed. One day he decided to ask his father if he could come inside, if he could go with his father to work, to see what it was like. And his father said he did not see why not, though he'd have to clear it first with the plant manager, a tieandshirt type of guy by the name of Russell Prescott. Which he did. And a date was set for that following Monday. And so, instead of getting ready to go to bed like he usually did at eleven o'clock, listening to the final innings of the Detroit Tigers game, the voice of Ernie Harwell drawling through the dimesized speaker on his transistor radio, he found himself walking the quarter of a mile upriver with his father, step by step in the darkness of this mid-July night, the sky frosted fly-ash gray with a haze that hung over in the wake of the day's ninety degree heat. His father didn't say anything the whole way there, though as they passed through the black-grated entry gates of Great Lakes Steel, he pushed his hand down into his front trouser pocket and pulled out two tiny tablets of salt: white like plain aspirin. "You think it's hot out here," his father warned. "Just wait until we get inside." And his father dropped the pills into his hand. It was true. Inside, the heat made it hard for him to breathe. The hot metal was so bright, it was so black with light, he could barely stand to watch as it drained from the blast furnace down to the thermo ladle waiting below. He closed his eyes, held in his breath. But still he could see the sudden flash of molten sparks showering down, could taste the burn of cooked limestone slag, could feel the calloused hand of his father reaching out toward him, taking hold of him, turning him away from the light.

WILLIAM MATTHEWS

Scorpio

You are unpredictable, obsessed by sex and death, eager to assert your individuality. You can be devious, but charming. You will not be invited to the party. You carry your young on your back, because your tail cannot reach there and, instinctively, they know that. You wish they would get off.

If you were born today, you would have been a great basketball player except for the accident. Today's Scorpio daughter will be beautiful and intense: when her wishes are granted, she's in trouble.

When two of you are gathered in my name, your tails will snarl in the air like incestuous lariats. You should take care of that pressing financial obligation today. You have forgotten something. What do you think it is? You are a spine whose legs have failed to evolve into ribs.

Your conversation is only about you: you never mention me. I am the one who made you what you are. It is my fault. Tonight should be devoted to romantic pursuits. Whom shall we chase? We will not be invited to the party. You ought to forget about me. You tend to be careless of others. You are the only one I have ever loved.

Sleeping Alone

A man is a necessity. A girl's mother says so by the way her hands come together after certain conversations, like a diary being closed.

But a boy's mother tells him a woman is a luxury. Maybe when he graduates his mother hugs him and forgets herself, she bites his earlobe! She remembers the hockey skates she gave him for Christmas when he was eight; the stiff flaps in back of the ankles resembled monks' cowls. The year before, the road froze over—they seemed to be what he should want.

Meanwhile the girl grows older, she hasn't been eight for ten years, her father is cruel to her mother. She'll always have a man, the way she likes to have in her room, even when visiting, a sandalwood box for her rings and coins, and a handpainted mug showing two geese racing their reflections across a lake.

Maybe she will meet the boy, maybe not. The story does not depend on them. In a dark room a couple undress. She has always liked men's backs and holds on with her fingertips, like suction cups, turning one cheek up to him and staring through the dark across the rippled sheet. He breathes in her ear—some women like that. Or maybe they've loved each other for years and the lights are on. It doesn't matter; soon they will be sleeping.

Why do we say we slept with someone? The eyelids fall. It isn't the one you love or anyone else you recognize who says the only words you will remember from the dream. It must be the dream speaking, or the pope of all dreams speaking for the church. It says, *It's OK, we're only dying.*

Jay Meek

Roadside Motels

I like to stop at motels built when tourists believed in cars the way they believed in safaris. There are motels steaming on the veldt, and motels shaded under the baobabs; some motels for the timid, and some for the assured. There are stucco motels where elephants pull in slowly, and motels for yaks, beatific and lascivious. There are family motels the wildebeests swim for, thousands of them crossing a river. Maybe an alligator strikes, or babies get trampled, but still the old bulls keep rising up the bank as if they saw the neon sign that spelled everything out: "Folks are Welcome Here." That's the roadside motel we're all heading for, clean rooms and cable TV where no one asks anything except an honest address, and where we can wake up the next day and look out at a field of antelopes grazing in the mist.

CHRISTOPHER MERRILL

Rosehips

for Marvin Bell

This false fruit, tear-shaped and smooth as a glass eye, cracks like pottery fired too quickly in a kiln. It reddens as it ripens, a line of yellow blearing. It's the smallest bird cage: inside, surrounded by an ocher sponge on the verge of rotting, are seeds and wings that soaked up sunlight in the thistles; freed, they flutter among the lodgepole pines at the pasture's edge, they float into the grass trampled by the horses that vanished in the night. Five leaves sprout from the pod, like the eyebrows of a woman who will travel constantly, in a small community. Rainwater on the leaves, and on the exposed roots of a dying aspen—a squirrel that skimmed across the pasture, like a stone. If you try to uproot the rose, you will shred your hands—the sharp thorns are thickest on the greying stems and branches near the base; only the green wood at the top is safe for stroking, though even here an emerging thorn may hook your finger.

What can you catch now that the horses are gone? The way they bolted through the open gate, followed a trail into the woods, and galloped up a canyon no one has ever explored. . . . Or else the water trough coated with pine needles, two feed bins steeped in falling leaves, a rusted chain girdling the aspen, a fence built by the woman who cares for injured raptors and burrowing owls, a glimpse of circus animals in a caravan of clouds encircled by a rainbow, clumps of a wildflower about to burst out of its buskins to cure the vision of a myopic child—the boy who rolls these pods, like marbles, across the ground, and watches the squirrel watching him.

Letters of Farewell (I)

Dear X,

We will not meet again—that much is clear from my last conversation with your family—and since this letter may not reach you in time or, if it does, may not coax you from the depths you are exploring with the single-mindedness of the scholar who refuses to share the fruits of his discovery, I write in the belief that words matter, even if they are never articulated in the presence of the living. This much we learned on our journey through Persia, when everything changed between us.

We should have stopped. True, it was too dark to see beyond what the lights of our borrowed car revealed, and our fear of the bandits hiding in the mountains led us to drive too fast for safety. Through the open windows we heard the howling of wild dogs or jackals, a gunshot, a muffled noise we could not name. There was no time to swerve when a face suddenly appeared before us—just the thud of the car striking a figure in the dark. Was it a bandit? Somebody in need of help? Neither of us said a word. And when you pressed down on the accelerator I nodded, although you couldn't see me.

The rest of the journey was eventless. When we returned the car, the owner said nothing about the dented bumper, accepting our extravagant tip with a benign smile. We took his advice to leave the country directly—the student demonstrations were gathering momentum—and it was not long before our government broke off diplomatic relations with theirs, leaving us in the clear. Nor did we ever discuss what happened that night.

The cooling of our friendship was no doubt inevitable. Years passed; and if on the occasions that brought us together we seemed outwardly devoted to each other, trading jokes and gossip, we understood our bond for what it was—an essay in erasure. We wanted to believe that we had driven through the night in a strange land about to fissure, where we were granted an intimation of what was coming.

But in fact we saw nothing more than a face, which sometimes rises up before my eyes, when I am dropping off to sleep or drunk on wine, to tell me in a strangled voice that we are not absolved. I suspect you reached the same conclusion. Hence your refusal to return my phone calls once it became clear that time was running out.

I wish I knew her name. Perhaps you know it now.

Yours,

Christopher Merrill

Lawrence Millman

Moon/Snail/Sonata

Newfoundland

I hoisted my anchor and raised the canvas and sailed off to a broken-down North Atlantic town. There I fasted on the precision of solitude. For hours or years, hard to say which, I'd sit and gaze at barnacles, trying to find one that was legendary. Occasionally I'd stick a finger into an anemone's soft ciliated slit—a destitute mating.

When I landed, I was all flotsam. Maybe a little jetsam, too. Then one moonlit night I went down to the sea. The sand had been exposed by the tide, and I could hear a low crustaceal breathing above the tumult of the waves.

I found myself walking among the barrows and sand collars of moon snails. I bent down and picked up one of the globular shells. The furrowed foot, sequined with sand, was twice the size of its thick ashen shell. In its slow writhing, it seemed like an archaic brain. Its scent was briny and seductive, like certain flesh.

The moon snail possesses a monolithic energy for shutting itself off. It will not leave home even to die. You can't see its secret parts, see all of it whole, while it's still alive. And so when I touched the snail's outstretched foot, it withdrew into its whorled sanctuary with a flush of hostile water. The operculum, a great brown eye, now stared me in the face: cheeky bastard, it seemed to say.

Here I was, a late Pleistocene trespasser in the demesne of a Triassic survivor. There was nothing for me to do but give back my moon snail to the cadence of the tides. So I put it softly down in the sand-edged foam, and it became a polished gem, a sapphire, the moment a wave rolled over its shell. See how nice I look (it seemed to say) without the benefit of your touch.

In the Westfjords of Iceland

This is the ultimate place, a narrow inlet gnarled like a sheep's gut and blue glacial battlements sawed off down to the sea, all of a bareness and purity that will never riot into flower. Blades of quicksilver surf chisel to grit a shingle gray with the brains of basalt. Avalanches hurl a slow music at each other and board with boulders the windows of the earth. Everything is stone and adamant except:

The flotsam bones of birds. Tangled in the maidenhair of moss or strung up in fisherman's twine. Frail cages flexed to grotesque angles, as finespun as spider's floss. A bleached, open beak resting on a shakedown of dulse. A head with saltwidened eyeholes. Wingbones—torn from whose body? Stray feathers shiver in the east wind, and then with the north wind dissolve. All that remains is the delicacy of dismemberment.

These bones are the toys of extinction, my dear. Touch them. In this boreal place, grant them your small momentary warmth. Spread your fingers along their pale brittle surfaces. Untie the twine. Deliver these lost armatures of being from their obscure destiny. For it is only through your grasp that they will rise up and speak to you:

"We are the mad ones who haunt your comfortable night. Across every known sea we have journeyed so that you might witness us stripped bare of all decoration. We come from Babi Yar and Treblinka, from Rwanda and the extremities of sleep. We lost our wings in El Salvador and East Timor. In Auschwitz, our lords and masters washed their faces with the skin of our skin. In the Gulags, they bottled our breath in the frozen earth. But we have escaped such geography, jettisoned so much, that we might reach this fastness in the western fjords. Let not our travels be futile, my dear."

Gabriela Mistral

The Lark

You said that you loved the lark more than any other bird because of its straight flight toward the sun. That is how I wanted our flight to be.

Albatrosses fly over the sea, intoxicated by salt and iodine. They are like unfettered waves playing in the air, but they do not lose touch with the other waves.

Storks make long journeys; they cast shadows over the Earth's face. But like albatrosses, they fly horizontally, resting in the hills.

Only the lark leaps out of ruts like a live dart, and rises, swallowed by the heavens. Then the sky feels as though the Earth itself has risen. Heavy jungles below do not answer the lark. Mountains crucified over the flat-lands do not answer.

But a winged arrow quickly shoots ahead, and it sings between the sun and the Earth. One does not know if the bird has come down from the sun or risen from the Earth. It exists between the two, like a flame. When it has serenaded the skies with its abundance, the exhausted lark lands in the wheatfield.

You, Francis, wanted us to achieve that vertical flight, without a zigzag, in order to arrive at that haven where we could rest in the light.

You wanted the morning air filled with arrows, with a multitude of care-free larks. Francis, with each morning song, you imagined that a net of golden larks floated between the Earth and the sky.

We are burdened, Francis. We cherish our lukewarm rut: our habits. We exalt ourselves in glory just as the towering grass aspires. The loftiest blade does not reach beyond the high pines.

Only when we die do we achieve that vertical flight! Never again, held back by earthly ruts, will our bodies inhibit our souls.

The Coconut Palms

We immediately recognize the coconut palms; they cannot be counted. For each dead Indian, the Spaniard planted a live palm, remaking the landscape, just as the race was remade in order to forget the former island, the home of Indians.

For forty days of my life, my eyes absorbed this new sky striped with vegetable necks, grooved with a million palm trees. A type of loom makes the warp, and allows the songs of birds and crazy insects to place the invisible weft, so rich with life.

After this, other skies will seem naked, devoid of the sovereign botanical core. The coconut palms are in a procession from Panateneas, a nomadic mass of coconut palms has created high ground with an unknown, orderly plan: palms united in a familiar party, exchanging friendly gestures. They touch heads and draw back their bodies. They dream with a tall hardness, but a melody always results below because of the longhaired heads bumping into each other, above.

Translated by Maria Giachetti.

Pablo Neruda

The Sand

These sands of yellow granite are unique, insurmountable. (The white sand, the black sand, adhere to the skin, to the clothing, they are impalpable and intrusive.) The golden sands of Isla Negra are formed like tiny spheres of rock, as if they originated in some demolished planet, which burned far away, up there remote and yellow.

Everyone walks across the sandy shore and crouches, searching, picking through the sand, to such an extent that someone called this coast "the Island of Lost Things."

The ocean is an incessant provider of half-rotted planks, balls of green glass or cork floats, fragments of bottles ennobled by rough seas, detritus of crab shells, conch shells, limpets, objects that have been eaten away, aged by pressure and insistence. It lives among brittle fish skeletons, miniscule sea urchins or purple crabs, serpentine *cochayuyo*, nourishment of the poor—interminable seaweed, round as an eel that slides and shines, made to quiver even on the sand by the reticent wave, by the ocean which pursues it. It's well known that this sea plant is the longest on the planet, growing to a length of four hundred meters, attached to the rocks by titanic suction, maintaining itself with a division of floaters which sustain the tresses of the macrocystis algae with thousands of little amber nipples. And since the condor flies over the Andean region and all the families of the albatross glide in for their reunions on the Chilean waters and survive here, we are a small homeland of very large wings, of very long tresses tossed by the great ocean, of shadowy presences in the great vaults of the sea.

The Stones

Stones, boulders, crags . . . Perhaps they were fragments of a deafening explosion. Or stalagmites that were once submerged, or hostile fragments of the full moon, or quartz that changed destiny, or statues that time and the wind broke into pieces or kneaded into shapes, or figureheads of motionless ships, or dead giants that were transmuted, or golden tortoises, or imprisoned stars, or ground swells as thick as lava which suddenly became still, or dreams of the previous earth, or the warts of another planet, or granite sparks that stood still, or bread for furious ancestors, or the bleached bones of another land, or enemies of the sea in their bastions, or simply stone that is rugged, sparkling, grey, pure and heavy so that you may construct, with iron and wood, a house in the sand.

Translated by Dennis Maloney and Clark M. Zlotchew.

Kristy Nielsen

Self-Portrait as My Father

What does it take? I know how to wire a room, to stop an elevator in flight, to go hunting and bring home a puppy instead of a dead duck, I know when to lick the syrup off the plate and when to set down my knife and clean my teeth with a toothpick and listen

so talk already, tell me all about yourself, every little thing

I could tell you a story if you want to hear your old man ramble. Once there was a girl who couldn't cry no matter what and she grew to be a woman with buckets of tears inside, a huge woman who shook the ground when she walked and trembled the trees, a real fatty fatty two by four—can you hear me? You got potatoes in your ears? Scrub harder spud farmer

and listen up because it gets really funny. One day the woman goes walking in the woods, trips and falls across a stream bed, blocks the water, creates a dam, the water swells and pools and everything washed downstream piles up against her, trees and shoes, beer cans, shopping carts, parts of cars, waterlogged stuffed animals, amazing, all this stuff you didn't think was around anymore

all surrounding this woman who couldn't cry. She asked to be left alone so she could die, but instead the people came and took pictures.

Naomi Shihab Nye

Hammer and Nail

"Would you like to see where our little girl is buried?" my friend asks as we walk between stucco shrines and wreaths of brilliant flowers. Even a plane's propeller is attached to a pilot's grave as if the whole thing might spin off into the wind. One man's relatives built a castle over his remains, with turrets and towers, to match the castle he built for his body in life. If you stand at a certain angle you can see both castles at once, the bigger one he lived in off on the horizon. An archway says in Spanish, "Life is an illusion. Death is the reality. Respect the dead whom you are visiting now." We hike down the hill toward the acres of "free graves." Here people can claim any space they want without paying, but also risk having someone buried on top of them. In the fields beyond the cemetery, women walk slowly with buckets slung over their shoulders on poles. Black cows graze on kneehigh grass. The crossbar from the marker to my friend's child's grave has come loose and lies off to one side. My friend kneels, pressing the simple blue crossbar back into the upright piece, wishing for a hammer and nail. The cross has delicate scalloped edges and says nothing. No words, no dates. It reminds me of the simplicity of folded hands, though I know there were years of despair. My friend says, "Sometimes I am still very sad. But I no longer ask, What if . . .?' It was the tiniest casket you ever saw." On the small plots in either direction, families have stuck tall pine branches into dirt. The needles droop, completely dried by now, but they must have looked lovely as miniature forests for the first few days.

La Feria

Here comes the woman who never looks up with one little girl riding her hip in a shawl and one slinking alongside. The man who fathered these babies is hard to find. He is usually sleeping with the woman he loved before this one who doesn't feel bad about it because she had him first. He is ugly but creative. He has designed buildings in town no one wants to enter because they feel heavy. The first woman says he will marry the second one sooner or later and that will be fine with her. If he says it is time. When the little girls ride a carnival car at La Feria they grip the steering wheel tightly and don't wave. All the other children circle round and round, smiling as the tiny breeze ruffles their hair. They are going on long trips, they say. But these two look grim as if they are staying in one place.

Nina Nyhart

Ghost Triptych

My mother's not dead yet, only wandering, not knowing if she's in one place or another. So she comes to sit beside me easily, more easily than in the past. And she disappears easily, as she often did. As I drive along, my mother's ghost flinches, shrinks from the savage traffic. What can you expect, I say, we're in Boston. Stoplight. She squirms impatiently. I remind her how lucky we are to be together, here, after so many years apart. She grows silent, and finally, as if love were the result of an algebraic equation she must work out, she agrees.

*

My father's ghost often visits my mother. He spends afternoons with her talking over the old days. He finds her no matter where she has wandered to—Philadelphia, the Gulf Coast—and today, on shipboard. Don't worry, she tells me over the phone, the ship is tied securely to the dock, and someone is cooking dinner. She's growing cold, though, the ship's in Alaska now—serious fishing—and so many men washed overboard. Such a harsh life, fishing.

*

I go to starlight as to a beautiful woman, my mother, wearing a long white silk jersey dress of the thirties, Hollywood style. She sits at the skirted dressing table before the triptych mirror combing her dark wavy hair. Three women open their lipsticks, apply crimson to their lips, dab Nuit de Noel on their throats. She puts on her diamond pin and earrings all shaped like stars. They sparkle in the dark room—starlight—and when I reach to touch it, it's gone, back into that darkness she shone from for a few minutes, long ago.

TOMMY OLOFSSON

Mortal Terror

These islands and skerries hiding in the rain, dampness and the start of fall stiffening my limbs. Even the grass bends down heavily today! Little birds hide themselves in the stone wall. No jackdaws congregate in the great oak. Where do they take shelter when it rains and gusts like this?

The sea is reveling, rolling in the surge of its senses. But the sky is boiling lead, a terribly melancholy soul; someone's provoked it to actions it would normally be appalled at.

There's a sorrow that cannot be fathomed. A weight that never turns solid enough to grasp. There's suffering that's dark and oppressive and strong. Every other feeling is drenched and blue with cold. The heart is an old tuber whose bruised blue eyes sleep in body tissue.

I am the root cellar that lies a little way off from the house I would most like to be. The leaky roofridge is my forehead. It feels as if I'll never be able to get on my feet again. The grave grows up along my walls. Like a creeper of earth and grass it reaches over me. Soon only the roof will show. And the door that springs open when someone turns the key, springing open with such force the hinges nearly fly off. Here I am, after all!

Cat Shadow

Like the shadow of a cat, darkness slinks into the room and brushes against my legs. The furniture crouches down, absorbed in its own upholstery. The books on their shelves press closer to each other.

Someone writes with darkness on my back. I've been sitting here so long I'd better get up from myself. I am only a temporary residence for my thoughts.

Silent swallows dart out of the walls to ghoststitch the twilight. Inside my skull, I start pacing off a grave for the day's burned-out thoughts. The cat's shadow looms a shroud.

Translated by Jean Pearson.

IMRE ORAVECZ

I Remember Clearly

the first time you came, you wore a short skirt, a transparent blouse, light sandals, your luggage was light as a feather, and you too were somehow light as a feather, sunny as the spring you came in, wide-awake, responsive to everything, and youthful, almost a child, and your body too almost a child's, downy and fresh, you told me in detail what the passport and customs inspection was like, what scenery you saw from the train window, how people treated you on the journey, and what it felt like to be in the eastern bloc for the first time, and you were surprised at what to me was unexceptional, and you found unexceptional what I was surprised at, you liked the city, you liked the old villas, the streets, the bridges, the confectioneries, the museums, the swimming pools, the police uniforms, the streetcars, and you tried ardently in bed to make up for what you missed in the meantime, and you always saw to it that I was pleased with everything, because you were pleased with everything, and you delighted in everything, in me, in yourself, in the world, and I remember clearly the last time you came, you wore a long two-piece suit, a bulky sweater, a pair of walking shoes, your luggage was heavy, and you too were somehow heavier and overcast as the fall you came in, withdrawn, already indifferent to certain things, and older, a real woman, and your body too a real woman's, mature and tired, you made no mention of what the passport and customs inspection was like, what scenery you saw from the train window, how people treated you on the journey, and what it felt like to be in the eastern bloc once again, you were no longer surprised at what to me was unexceptional, and you did not find unexceptional what I was surprised at, you were indifferent to the city, unmoved by the old villas, the streets, the bridges, the confectioneries, the museums, the swimming pools, the police uniforms, and you no longer tried so ardently in bed to make up for what you'd missed in the meantime, and you did not always see to it that I was pleased with everything, because

Robert Perchan

Nights at the Races

He believed in a kind of metempsychosis, a transmigration of souls, that when he made bareback love to a woman in the solitude of his cabin all his dead male ancestors would show up and gather around the bed to cheer on the sperm carrying their own personal code. In the mornings the place would be a mess, littered with tote-machine tickets that had been ripped in half and the butt-ends of fat stogies that had been dropped or tossed away during an exhilarating dead-heat finish. And, sometimes, when he and the woman swept up, they would come across one of last night's losers, some dimly-remembered black sheep, some dead-end lush who had died without issue, huddled in a corner under an overcoat stained with vomit. And then, with charity in their hearts, he would don a condom and they would slip back under the blankets and knock one off just for such-like lost souls, the unbegetters, the true wand'ring Shades, the eternally stopped.

Francis Ponge

The Pleasures of the Door

Kings do not touch doors.

They know nothing of this pleasure: pushing before one gently or brusquely one of those large familiar panels, then turning back to replace it—holding a door in one's arms.

The pleasure of grabbing the midriff of one of these tall obstacles to a room by its porcelain node; that short clinch during which movement stops, the eye widens, and the whole body adjusts to its new surrounding.

With a friendly hand one still holds on to it, before closing it decisively and shutting oneself in—which the click of the tight but well-oiled spring pleasantly confirms.

The Frog

When little matchsticks of rain bounce off drenched fields, an amphibian dwarf, a maimed Ophelia, barely the size of a fist, sometimes hops under the poet's feet and flings herself into the next pond.

Let the nervous little thing run away. She has lovely legs. Her whole body is sheathed in waterproof skin. Hardly meat, her long muscles have an elegance neither fish nor fowl. But to escape one's fingers, the virtue of fluidity joins forces with her struggle for life. Goitrous, she starts panting. . . And that pounding heart, those wrinkled eyelids, that drooping mouth, move me to let her go.

Translated by Beth Archer Brombert.

CRISTIAN POPESCU

Tradition

Ever since the No. 26 trolley began running, my family has reserved this very seat in this very car. Look at the little plaque with our family name. Here is where my father always sat, here is where my grandfather sat. They would sit motionless with a ticket in their hand, with a smile on their lips. Now it's my turn. Now I'm the one who maintains the collection of picture postcards of all the stops the 26 makes along its route. From my father I learned to paint the window every once in a while with clear nail polish to brighten the views.

When I decide to get off and see my wife, I place a manikin on my seat, a likeness of me, and I stick the ticket between its fingers. A manikin dressed in my wedding suit. And when I return, I find lipstick smeared on its cheeks from the young ladies who dare not kiss me in the flesh. Each night I bring my wife and children to the depot, I help them onto the car, and, perched on the driver's seat, I turn the crank and clang the trolley's bell on the hour until the first pale light of dawn.

Translated by Adam J. Sorkin and Bogdan Stefanescu.

Yannis Ritsos

Evening Walk

Houses have their secrets. They signal back and forth by means of colors, carvings, windows, anthemions, chimneys in the most unlikely and suggestive postures. Stepping out my door, I catch them talking in whispers. They immediately fall silent, and their facades turn serious, as if a stranger had barged in on an intimate gathering. They wear the displeased expression of a man interrupted while drinking his tea, the hand holding the teacup arrested a little below chin-level. Just so the streets. No sooner do they see me coming than they hurriedly seal up their secrets, now under the traffic lights at the corner, now under the few pepper trees, now in the shadow of a parked truck. They remind me of the huge buffet in the house I grew up in. It was always kept locked. Behind the fine cut glass, which reflected the bright squares of the windows in miniature, I could sense the delicate liqueur glasses, the little silver spoons that were brought out only for special guests, a giant fork for serving caviar, the porcelain, the jars full of candied oranges, and something else, I don't remember, they never let me see it, on the top shelf, I was so small I couldn't reach that high, not even the time I pulled over a chair and climbed up, one afternoon when mother was out and they'd left the buffet unlocked. "Good evening, Ariosto, how are you?" I hear an oddly gentle voice. It's a colleague from the office. His voice feels sorry for me. I can see in his eyes how sad and unshaven I look. The sunset flashes on balcony railings and in windows, at once lugubrious and magnificent. And I am like a man whose wife left him the day before, and he walks the street knowing that his house is locked, that its rooms are empty, that a fine layer of dust is forming along the backs of the furniture, and all that's left, on the arm of the sofa, are her worn, tan gloves, which she forgot at the last moment. Yet the evening spills over with colors—yellow, pink, cobalt, deep purple, and a gold

VERN RUTSALA

Carpe Diem

This morning he knows exactly what he has to do—it is all very clear and so simple it surprises him—and he packs his gear with great care. He wears his freshly washed and starched fatigues and feels as sharp as he had in the army, boots spit-shined, belt buckle glistening. Moving briskly as he works he likes the ozone flavor of the autumn air and the pure blue sky which seems as clear as his plan. He thinks again of leaving a note on the fridge but knows his plan is far too complex to spell out in words however clear it seems to him. Later, his wife and kids will understand. The plan simmers just above his heart and he is dead certain that it is right. Today will be a great day.

In spite of having drunk malt liquor all night he feels sober, reflexes in perfect order, eyes and fingers in ideal harmony. He drives along his usual route, not speeding, enjoying the light traffic and the purring gurgle of his pickup at stop lights. He thinks of his job, remembering those abstract motions, that lifting, bending and rising, the dance that danced its mania into him is gone now, invisible. He feels no anger about it. They'll understand. He takes it as a good omen when he finds a parking slot easily and at the time clock he loads a clip and slips the safety off and decides to hell with the foreman and just opens fire.

Sleeping

Though winners are rarely declared this is an arduous contest similar, some feel, to boxing. This fact can be readily corroborated by simply looking at people who have just awakened. Look at their red and puffy eyes, the disheveled hair, the slow sore movements, and their generally dazed appearance. Occasionally, as well, there are those deep scars running across their cheeks. Clearly, if appearances don't lie, they have been engaged in some damaging and dangerous activity and furthermore have come out the losers. If it's not dangerous—and you still have doubts—why do we hear so often the phrase, He died in his sleep?

Holy Day

And things were going so well—you winning the drawing, me getting the raise as our team soars to the top, the screaming almost gone. Ok, so I hit the kid again, he deserved it. Pain, tears, ice to the spot, but no bruise anyone could see. He's got to learn. Besides, he's fine now; I'm the one sick with it. Isn't this sadness enough? It could be an echo of the famous trial, wife beaten and murdered with her boyfriend, the killer set free. He's so sorry. We think it helped him to be famous. But the rest of us? The doctor injects the serum, we get tired, immunity breaks down, we're overcome. Cancel my subscription, turn off that popular song.

Avenu Malkenu: for the sin that I have sinned against thee: a day fasting, hope for another year, and better—don't you understand? Luckily, we've stopped expecting that.

CHARLES SIMIC

Heroic Moment

I went bare-assed into the battle. The President himself heard of my insolence. I was given a flea-ridden mutt to ride. I rode in company of crows pleading with them to please remember me. I had a dollhouse knife between my teeth, the red plastic pisspot on my head as a helmet.

When she heard the news, my mother caused the Greek fleet to be deprived of favorable winds on its way to Troy. Witch, they called her, dirty witch—and she, so pretty, chopping the onions, laughing and crying over the stew pot.

Voice from the Cage

Mr. Zoo Keeper, will you be making your rounds today? We are howling, we are clucking in distress. It's been ages since you've come. We smell awful, we smell to high heaven. Sorrow, sickness, and flea bites are our lot.

The rabbits still screw but their weakness is optimism. Even the lion doesn't believe the fables any more. "Pray to the Lord," the monkeys shriek. I've dyed my hair green like Baudelaire. The big circus tent, I tell everybody, still stands in the distance. I can see the trumpets glow. I can hear the snare drum.

Ours is a circus of quick, terrified glances.

GORAN SIMIC

Medals

When he returned from the war my grandfather locked himself up in the attic and did not come out for fifteen days. During the day he was silent and at night he would moan so terribly that the candles under the icon would go out. My grandmother saw the faces of death when he finally came down.

When my father returned from the war in his bloodstained overcoat, he spilled a heap of medals from his bag and went up to the attic without looking at anyone. During the day we would compare his medals with grandfather's, and at night we would put our heads under the pillows so as not to hear him calling his dead friends and moaning. Come morning, my mother would place his shiny medals on the window for passersby to see. But no one passed by our house anymore because no one could stand the moaning. One morning we found a ghost in the overcoat by the bed. The ghost watching with his own eyes.

It happened a long time ago. The family vault has thickened. The medals still hang on the walls, and sometimes the clerks take them during the holidays and return them after a couple of days. I would not even notice if they never returned them. Only sometimes, after I'm horrified by the news of the war, I see them on the wall. Because the only thing left from my father and grandfather are the screams and moans, and I console myself that it is the wind scratching the damaged attic beams of our simple house.

Translated by Amela Simic and Christopher Merrill.

Lennart Sjögren

The Barn

Through the crack in the wall they saw a dead person. The barn was high, it smelled faintly of last year's hay, in the morning the light fell in clearly. There was in fact only the one crack in the tightly-made wall where it was possible to peep through. A knot which had worked itself out of the edge of the plank widened the crack significantly. They were drawn there, looked in, looked at each other: there she lay. Two trestles, a sofa-lid, a white sheet, and the profile which was now so firm and uplifted. But the eyelids lay deep.

They looked at her and remembered her like this for the rest of their lives. When the one of them died, more than seventy years later, the other, the survivor, found himself thinking first of all not about the man who had just died but about the woman who lay straight and white in the clear morning inside the barn. And he saw her face.

After Sleep

He falls asleep in the afternoon. Meanwhile the clouds rise. When he wakens summer is past. The heat which made the grass wither and the wells dry up is past. The sky which was so blinding is past.

He goes out in the forest to see if the waterhole still holds water. He has been sleeping for only half an hour. The cows stand black beneath the foliage, they look hard at him. Can it really be that they know an age has vanished since the morning, is he a stranger to them, someone they would no longer acknowledge?

The metal of the car body is now harder and more silent than before, the faces mirrored in it are closed. And the houseroofs, whether tin or tile, have stored up within themselves an absence which makes the tongue dry.

Yet no great thunderstorm has drawn past. Only a cloud-back. It has given neither rain nor lightning. But the sleep came and worked a change. Out of the sea the fish call to him to come down there.

Everything is finlike, before the age of man.

Translated by Robin Fulton.

WILLIAM SLAUGHTER

China Lesson

What's he thinking, I'm thinking, the real live Panda Bear? As he rides his motorbike around the ring in the Shanghai Acrobatic Theater where he's a featured performer. With a look, an air, of complacency about him. He's thinking private thoughts. More than his trainer knows, who turns in the center of the ring pointing approvingly at the Panda Bear. The trainer is completely taken in. He believes the applause is for him. But the Panda Bear is nobody's fool. He has an above average IQ and a diploma from Panda Bear School. He has learned his China lesson well. His eyes, and the expression on his face, reveal nothing. Give nothing away. He's keeping it all in, saving it for himself. The Panda Bear has a secret. One night—tonight?—he's going to break the circle with his trainer still pointing approvingly at him and ride his motorbike out of the theater into the night. He knows exactly what he's doing. Who can stop him? The Panda Bear has done his homework. Has studied geography. The map of China is in his head as he rides south out of Shanghai toward the border crossing at Shenzhen. Panda Bears don't need passports to get into the New Territories and Hong Kong. They just go. He'll take up residence there in a small flat—in Stanley, say—and live a quiet life anonymously. Perhaps he'll have a stall on the waterfront where he'll sell small replicas of himself which he'll draw with brush and ink using his own right paw. Doing a tidy business. Smiling all the while. Never looking back.

Thomas R. Smith

Windy Day at Kabekona

Only a picture window stands between us and the full force of gusts that lift the branches of the red pine. Draft under the cabin door rolls the rug resolutely into a tube despite our attempts to lay it flat.

Foothigh waves spume across the lake; near shore the color of the long, gleaming swells softens to a milky jade, warmer looking than it is, almost southern. But the drift of this world is northerly; lawn chairs are hurled into woodpiles, propellers of outboard motors scrape against stones. The door bangs loosely in its sill. Jack pines groan as if they could snap and fall.

There is something in all this fury that makes the day oceanic: We're near at any moment being swamped, drowned, pinned by wreckage. In the cloudless sky, the sun gleefully conducts the turbulence as though it were Wagnerian opera. A gull white as our idea of angels hovers above the shore for a moment—fully awake—fighting the wind before being torn from its place.

Madelon Sprengnether

Necrophilia

In this movie a woman is in love with the body of death. She wants to smell, touch, taste it. She wants to puncture it, caressing the internal organs, watching the exchange of chemicals with blood. If she sings, dances, has sex with it, she will feel its whole history of hurt or joy. For such a thrill, she is willing to do anything. But this is fiction. Tonight, in Sally's kitchen, I hear a woman describe how she entered her mother's bedroom moments after her death. How the air in there was like mica, thin and flashing. Yet how warm and supple her mother's flesh. How she washed her, changed her nightgown, combed her hair. How she inhaled then, deeply and slowly. Taking into her lungs all the cutting edges of her life.

The Franklin Avenue Bridge

If I walk down to the river, on a near-freezing, near-thawing January day. If I walk close to sunset, with the river white and rigid at the edges, at the center black and flowing. If I walk through the hard and the slushy stuff, sometimes gripping, sometimes sliding. If I see three small boys coming home from school, their coats flapping open. If I nearly crash into one careening down a homemade toboggan run on his front lawn. If I cross the Franklin Ave. bridge, with the moon at my back like a premonition, the sky before a pulsing, radiant orange. If I stop, transfixed by all that is passing, racing or glowing. How will I know (if I love the light at this moment) who holds me (as much as the darkness that is to come) in the world's open palm?

Maura Stanton

Searches

Once again TV detectives are searching the suspects' rooms in some old rambling house in England. The Chief Inspector opens the bureau drawers in tiers, pulling out striped ties and folded white shirts; he sniffs every cut-glass bottle; he ruffles through papers on the desk, unclasps a small leather book and turns unerringly to the suspicious entry. In anther room his tweed-coated assistant pushes back filmy dresses, and holds up a black high heel, checking for traces of a red garden clay. "Why is there a dead wasp on the nightstand?" he wonders aloud, while his superior calls him across the hall. "Why has someone thrown a glass of brandy into the fireplace?" Red herrings, these questions will never be answered, but the two men exchange knowing looks as the musical score, something in imitation of Elgar, swells in excitement. Downstairs in a library of mullioned windows and walls of gilt-stamped books, the impatient suspects drink sherry and smoke cigarettes, their faces twitching, their eyes shifty or worried or insouciant. Later, alone here in my own room, I wonder if I have any secrets from myself, and I open my top drawer briskly to see who this person is who calls herself by my name. What's this? All these curious hair ornaments, barrettes, tortoise shell combs, silver elastic bands. Here's a snood; here are chiffon ribbons and satin ribbons; a box full of black bobby pins with blunt plastic tips and another containing thin sharp spidery hairpins; here's an ancient torn hairnet for blondes; here's an unopened package containing a nylon flexible comb tossed on top of jeweled pony-tail holders, a lime-plastic device for creating a French roll, a spongy nylon doughnut for a bun, and more barrettes, some cloisonné, others burnished metal. Oh how unerringly a detective's hands sort through this distracting clutter! The camera zooms in on a small box of "Bronchial-Pastillen" from the Hertenstein Drogerie in Lucerne, Switzerland. Throat lozenges or cyanide tablets? I'm as surprised as the audience when I pry open the tin lid to discover a cache of fifty yellowed slips saved from the centers of crisp fortune cookies devoured years ago in forgotten Chinese restaurants. What can it mean? The camera moves in on my expression. Another red herring? Or the real clue to her existence?

Eva Ström

The Unblessed

The unblessed broke a day out of the week and tasted it. It was white, indifferent. The edges of the day were riddled with thousands of small wormholes, only the core was healthy, a hard compressed piece of inaccessible time. Through this time nothing would pass, time wouldn't move but neither would it stand still. Time had become matter and like matter would grow old.

Huge Wings for a Frail Body

When day approached evening the dusk gathered round a pink doll's pram that stood parked among the columbines. The grass was high and the nightingale beat with his dull hard drills against the dense thicket. The child who had played with the doll's pram had grown up, it hadn't been able to see the open view of the dark one, the dead earth full of twigs and waste. What did it resemble? Huge wings for a frail body.

Translated by Robin Fulton.

JAMES TATE

All over the Lot

We were at the ballgame when a small child came up to me and thwacked me in my private area. He turned and walked away without a single word. I was in horrible pain for a couple of minutes, then I went looking for the rascal. When I found him he was holding his mother's hand and looking like the picture of innocence. "Is that your son?" I asked of the lady. She shot me a look that could fry eggs, and then she slapped me really hard. "Mind your own business," she screaked. The boy grinned up at me. My old tweed vest was infested with fleas. I started walking backwards. People were shoving me this way and that. To each I replied, "God, I love this game, I love this game."

Her Silhouette against the Alpenglow

Climbing a mountain is very hard work so we just sat at the bottom of it and ate our picnic. Others came along and actually started to climb it. They were tough and strong but we still thought they were foolish, but refrained from telling them so. They were loaded down with so much equipment they could barely walk on level ground—ropes, sleeping bags, tents, hammers, pitons, lamps, food supplies, ice axes, oxygen masks—whereas for a picnic you can get everything you need into a basket—wine, cheese, salami, bread, napkins. "Marie," I said, "Do you still love me?" "Chuck you, Farley," she said, "and your whole famn damily. You know I'll always love you. All's hotsie-dandy here, thank you very much."

CARINE TOPAL

Max in Egypt

Years ago, years ago, my mother and her mother left Dresden, city of goldrimmed porcelain and fine china cups, to take the train to another country, dip into the mud and mineral baths at Trencin Teplice. It was Czechoslovakia, 1933. There they would crouch and turn until the wet earth shrunk from the early sun and became their second skin.

Grandpa Max sailed to Egypt where he schooled darkhaired Fatimas in the art of western romance. He called all the girls Yasmine. It was the *khamsin*, time of the hot winds which left men, like grandpa, sipping mint tea, sucking the *nahna* until there was nothing but a withered mint leaf on his marblewhite left hand, because in his right, he held his cigarette, German style, index finger pointing, tapping ashes of the cigarettes he lit and handed out lavishly to young girls, girls from the province of Sawhaj, girls from towns with names that sang Zagzig, Akhim, Ismailia.

The tips of grandpa's index and mid-finger were saffron-yellow. And he pressed these fingers to take the pinky of one girl, any one, and he pressed these fingers to take the nipple of another and twist it in his mouth, then watch it return, glimmering from saliva. And the nipples, when dried and pink, had a yellow tinge too.

Grandpa Max lived an extraordinary life, drawn into the circle of glittering objects, snake charmers and transvestite dancers. The pleasure of female pursuit was here, in Cairo and Alexandria. Here, the smells of the souk—zatar and sesame—the endless carpets and billowing trousers floating from the walls. A boat ride down the Nile. Who would have known that in several years, Max's life would be a ship filled with Persian carpets, crystal chandeliers and all that fleeing Jews could carry.

ALISON TOWNSEND

Fever of Unknown Origin, 1955

At age two I nearly died, a fever of unknown origin sweeping me on dark swells while you floated, constant at my side. For six weeks you hovered, a blurred figure in a white gown with blue flowers, who leaned into my crib, crooning old songs I have never forgotten and praying, willing me into life again.

There was the touch of your hand on my cheek when they changed the i.v. in my ankle. And there was the knowledge that you slept beside me at night, a tall, blonde woman curled uncomfortably into the small cot at my side. Once I saw you leaning toward the window at twilight, staring into a sky starred gold by city lights. I thought I was dreaming, but you turned slowly, weeping, and somehow I realized, *She will be sad if I leave her. I must get better. I must come back from wherever I am.*

Years later, in the middle of Beethoven's Sixth Symphony, outdoors at the Hollywood Bowl, that same night sky opens above me and I hear you calling across time, across distance. *Come back, little girl,* you say. *Come back, my darling. Don't die. Please come back.* The wind lifts my hair, though the trees are not moving. In my adult life, sitting beside a man I love, I am three thousand miles from the place I last saw you, a woman walking out an arched door toward her own death in winter, white flakes swirling like an omen in her face.

It's summer, and I am far away. But your clear voice stretches like a rope from the land of the dead into the land of the living. It brings me back to the world, the way you brought me back as a sick child, the way you remind me to come back when I'm most tempted to give up and enter the kingdom of darkness. To come back because you are with me, though I'm no longer your little girl but a woman grown beyond you. To come back because you love me, because even half a lifetime later and one death between us, that is what remains.

A Child's Book of Death

I don't know who watched over your body, Mother, after you'd left it, or how my father got you from Cleveland to Dobbs Ferry. I only know that you arrived, motionless and as chill to the touch as the flesh of certain poisonous mushrooms. I was afraid of you then—though it seemed disloyal—and thought maybe I'd killed you, praying for you to die when you did not return as you'd promised.

Night after night, kneeling beside the spool bed, my pink flannel nightie with lambs tucked around my ankles, the floor breathing snaky drafts, the sisal carpet pricking my knees, I begged the great and implacable dark to make you better and bring you home, offering up Babar or Barbie the way I'd offered Raggedy Ann, on whom I operated, slitting her kapok-filled chest with nail scissors and digging my fingers in deep for her heart.

Which was supposed to be real, the way you were but then were not, as you lay before us, your body stuffed with darkness I smelled but couldn't see, the distance you'd traveled as enormous as all the states that slept between us while you lay dying in your high, white hospital bed, and Jenny and Steve and I prayed for you—*Our Father who art in heaven . . . Now I lay me down to sleep*—every prayer we knew, our words a useless gabble we wanted to be true, falling from the small, mint-scented churches of our mouths.

Tomas Tranströmer

Madrigal

I inherited a dark wood where I seldom go. But a day will come when the dead and the living change places. Then the wood will start moving. We are not without hope. The most serious crimes will remain unsolved in spite of the efforts of many policemen. In the same way there is somewhere in our lives a great unsolved love. I inherited a dark wood, but today I'm walking in the other wood, the light one. All the living creatures that sing, wriggle, wag and crawl! It's spring and the air is very strong. I have graduated from the university of oblivion and am as empty-handed as the shirt on the washing-line.

Translated by Robin Fulton.

The Cuckoo

A cuckoo sang in a birch tree just north of the house. It was so loud that at first I thought it was an opera singer imitating a cuckoo. Surprised I saw the bird. Its tailfeathers moved up and down with each note like a pump handle. The bird hopped, turned around, and screamed to every point of the compass. Then it lifted into the air and flew over the house and far to the west, cursing under its breath . . . The summer grows old, everything flows together and forms a single melancholy whisper. *Cuculus canorus* returns to the tropics. Its time in Sweden is over. It didn't last long! In fact, the cuckoo is a citizen of Zaire. . . . I am no longer fond of traveling. But the journey visits me. Now that I'm being pushed farther into a corner, now that the tree-rings multiply and I need reading glasses. What happens is always more than we can carry. There's nothing to be surprised about. These thoughts carry me as faithfully as Susi and Chuma carried Livingstone's mummified corpse through Africa.

Translated By Michael McGriff.

Mark Vinz

Letter from the Cabin

for Jay and Martha

I've watched all week, but it seems the eagles really haven't returned this year. The heron's nest on the other side of the inlet is deserted, too, though high water and tricky winds make it impossible to get out in the boat most days. Still, it's enough to look up from whatever page I'm turning and watch the lake—the long trajectory of loons skimming the water, wings beating waves, echoing cries. You know how they always thrill us, especially at night.

It's humid today, the thick clouds seeming to grow from the shore— when friends are here, it's what we scarcely notice, up late, talking quietly on the screened-in porch. In the morning there is always time to take turns stretching out on the dock, to be alone with birds and sky and water. And now, as dinner wine is cooling in the refrigerator, you're here again, all of us peering out into the fading light, amazed by wind in leaves, full of smiles for this other life—the one where we're totally thankful.

The Getaway

He's been like this for days, ever since we got here—just sitting there in front of the porch screen staring at the lake, watching the shifting wind ripple the water, the sunlight on the leaves. He waves to every passing boat, every bird. "Loon," he cries. "Crow, mallard, great blue heron!" To tell the truth, we're starting to get worried. "I'm going to order some binoculars," he calls out, "and a canoe just like that one. I wonder if it comes in green."

We even have to bring him dinner on a tray, out there in the fading light where he's cheering the squirrels and chipmunks. And now, when it's too dark to see anymore, he's made a bed out of blankets and pillows. We can hear him most of the night—flat on his back, dozing, watching above his toes. "Firefly," he shouts. "Shooting star!"

Liz Waldner

Post Prandial

for SweetBee Smoothfield

Time, fine, a fine time was had by all. The tine of the fork, the fork of the tree, the tree of life, the life of Reilly and now it's either Irish or smiley. Eyes, nays, *pince nez,* sweat bee. A sweat bee reconnoitering me. The cicada sound swells and dies like the sea on the sand, like the breeze in the trees. The bee's still reconnoitering me. An orange-edged winged thing flies by fast. The band about my brain tightens. The buzz saw, the band saw, song of some bug, and the sweat bee lands on my blue muumuu, probes to be sure it's missing nothing sweet. Its eyes attuned to another frequency, it can't be sure. Me, neither. SweetBee, hello. I am fickle. Something stung me at yesterday evening's dinner party. It left a welt like missing you.

Rosmarie Waldrop

This

When the medulla oblongata is pricked, or in any other way irritated, the white furious sun high in a state of tension. Shed her clothes and inexplicably married. Caught in the fact. The first representations of Amerindians showed naked men and women gnawing on a human leg with equal opportunity. Her husband avoided looking directly into her face.

While nervous power is necessary to muscular motion the sun cannot be replaced by logic. Hence the inhabitants of New England have never made friends without blinds drawn. Solitary muscles, such as the sphincter, are always contracted. The Indians stood between quotation marks. While an oblique ray of sunlight penetrates a silk blouse the stimulus is shown as consistent. In all his life, he had seen nothing that so delighted his parts.

Likewise, a quick thrust on the toepad excites language and a shade too sure of herself. Subcutaneous itch. To fight it out in whispers, in degrees Fahrenheit. Desire flaked off the shoulder of the highway, by way of blaming the sun. To introduce difference into the all-or-nothing theory, the women wore no covering other than a narrow cloth over their privates. A heavy penetrating odor caught on the person of her husband.

The sun's influence on nerves, though in small quantities, the angle of incidence sealing cooperation and paraphrase. As nature intended, there was hair on the rest of his body. In the upper half of the picture, the condition of sight itself. The longer the Indians stood in the sun, the more it turned their eyes back into their body. This was before she knew she was pregnant.

CHARLES HARPER WEBB

Pomades

The chairman of a university physics department develops "quite a thing" for pomades.

He doesn't mention it to anyone. Not even in bed to his pretty blonde wife twelve years his junior. Not even in his backyard, playing badminton with his good-looking kids, a girl and a boy, ten and twelve years old respectively, who do well in school, have lots of nice friends, and are perfectly adjusted.

He denies the "thing" to himself. He denies even the need to deny having denied it. He in no way ever, not for one split second, indicates the presence of the "thing." It's just as if the "thing" does not exist.

Except it does.

In the lecture hall; in the laboratory; at the beach playing frisbee; at the symphony hearing Beethoven brutalized; at the laundromat washing his hunting pants and his wife's panties the day their washer broke; at the podium chairing the biggest convention of internationally-renowned physicists ever; relaxing in his chaise longue on his fresh-cut lawn on summer evenings, watching pretty girls bounce by in tans and shorts and halter-tops—loving his wife, and reflecting that life has been good to him.

Pomades.

Oh sweet Jesus, pomades.

Tom Whalen

Baseball

The games we played as children! The way the birds screeched at sunset and the earth swallowed the sun! Then Timmy would begin to cry and Billy would comfort him by whispering into his ear the names of forgotten short-stops and we would hide in the tall grass of the outfield with our gloves over our mouths. Always our summer days would end this way with the playing field scarred and our bats in splinters and our heads longing for the stars that soon would appear and form the constellation of Mother calling us inside. But we, with our warm breath and bones, did not want to return to our homes, we wanted to play on and on until the baseball broke apart like a dandelion, and the leaves fell, and the snows fell, and the air . . .

PETER WORTSMAN

The Riddle of the Sphinx

Sometimes, sound asleep, she lets out cries, fetal and almost unutterable, rousing you into sudden listening. The riddle of the sphinx must have been posed like this—howled—moaned—wept. You listen intently for an instant, try to decipher the inconsolable hieroglyphs, then embrace her without thinking. Shadow of a bird of prey passing, the unnamed sadness dissolves—in silence—or sometimes is repeated in the deafening howl of a delivery truck stalled in early morning traffic.

James Wright

The City of Evenings

The word evening has always seemed beautiful to me, and surely Venice is the city of evenings. It is renowned everywhere for its dawns, when the cathedrals and basilicas take solid shape out of the milky pearl. But their solidity is stone, even the finest of stone, the delicate sea-washed rippled marble floated here from Constantinople. It is only the evenings that give the city the shape of light; they make the darkness frail and they give substance to the light.

It is still too early for evening, and the smoke of early September is gathering on the waves of the Giudecca Canal outside my room. Steamers, motorboats, trash-scows are moving past in large numbers, and gondolas are going home. In a little while we too will meet the twilight and move through it on a vaporetto toward the Lido, the seaward island with its long beach and its immense hotel, its memories of Aschenbach and his harrowing vision of perfection, of Byron on horseback in the moonlight, and the muted shadows of old Venetians drifting as silently as possible in flight from the barbarians, drifting as far away as the island of Torcello, taking refuge as Ruskin said like the Israelites of old, a refuge from the sword in the paths of the sea. Maybe Torcello was nothing much for the princess of the sea to find, but the old Venetians discovered the true shape of evening, and now it is almost evening.

(Venice)

The Fruits of the Season

It is a fresh morning of late August in Padova. After the night's rain, the sun is emerging just enough so far to begin warming the grapes, melons, peaches, nectarines, and the other fruits that will soon fill this vast square. Women and children in bright flower-print dresses are already beginning to amble from stall to stall.

At the very far end of the square I can see the azure and golden face of the town clock on the Torre dell'Orologio.

A baker with white flour sprinkled all over his boots just drifted across the extreme right corner of my eye.

It is all commonplace, ordinary, the firm shaping of the morning in an Italian city of middling size.

And yet—to my left I can see the entire front length of the Palazzo della Ragione, on whose second floor the community has arranged a huge exhibit of paintings, the enduring fruits of five hundred years.

And spread below the faces of those peculiarly tender and fierce angels, the men and women and their children are still arriving from the country-side, arranging for our slow ambling choice the heaps of grapes, melons, peaches, nectarines, and all the other fruits of the season in a glory that will not last too long.

But they will last long enough. I would rather live my life than not live it. The grapes in a smallish stall are as huge and purple as smoke. I have just eaten one. I have eaten the first fruit of the season, and I am in love.

(Padua)

DAVID YOUNG

Lullaby for the Elderly

Under the hum and whir of night, under the covers, deep in the bed, beyond all the calling of doves, past the great flares of love and pain, the daily bread and grind, it's warm as a pot, soft as a breast. It's the deep woods, the place where you come to a clearing, find the still pool, and slip gently into it—to bathe, to dive, to drown.

Your mother is there, under the leaves, smelling of milk, and your father is hiding among the trees. A giant hand tousles your hair, and the mouse is there with its dangerous eyes, the bear with his shimmering fur, the rivers that thunder off ledges and spill into gorges as mist.

When you wake, refreshed, murmur a blessing for those who have never returned. Say a word to the corn and the wheat, to the deer and squirrels and whistling toads, who brought you right up to the edge of the woods and let you go in on your own.

GARY YOUNG

I discovered a journal in the children's ward, and read, I'm a mother, my little boy has cancer. Further on, a girl has written, this is my nineteenth operation. She says, sometimes it's easier to write than to talk, and I'm so afraid. She's offered me a page in the book. My son is sleeping in the room next door. This afternoon, I held my whole weight to his body while a doctor drove needles deep into his leg. My son screamed, Daddy, they're hurting me, don't let them hurt me, make them stop. I want to write, how brave you are, but I need a little courage of my own, so I write, forgive me, I know I let them hurt you, please don't worry. If I have to, I can do it again.

My son is learning about death, about the possibilities. His cat was killed. Then Mark died, then Ernesto. He watched the news, and saw soldiers bulldozed into the earth after battle. Down the road, a boy his age was found floating in a pond. My son says, we're careful about water, and splashes in his own warm bath. We don't want to die, he says, we want to live forever. We only just die later, he says, and nods his head. Death is comprehensible; what comes later is a week away, or two, and never arrives.

GENIE ZEIGER

The Hole

Today I ironed a woolen shawl, which a woman in Calcutta spent six months embroidering. She sold it for a song because the buyer, my ex-husband, found three moth holes at one end. I'd never bargain with that woman, I'd never offer her fewer rupees because of a few small holes.

The hole in the shawl is the hole in the screen that lets the flies in, is the hole in the world through which people come and go, is the "luch in kup" my father ascribed to the truly dumb. The rabbit scurries into it, the snake; it is the space between the rocks through which the sheep flee, through which the world enters, shyly at first, then brazenly.

The hole is the proverbial eye of the needle, the gap between teeth, the rip through which the dead return with their old coats and hats, with the sound of feet stamping to loosen the dust.

Mend it, fill it, glut it, wet it, stitch it, paste it, stuff it with vowels, consonants, entire dictionaries, and nothing works. What can you do? There's the hole. How can you fit into that tiny space gracefully, then live in it with so little room?

Woman on a Chessboard

after a photo by Edward Judice

The ground below me has grown hard and meticulous, a field of angles, a patchwork of black and white, clearly delineated, but nothing pure about it, the dark full of lesser dark, the white riddled by the less than white. Standing here, I am Electra after she finally finished wailing over her brother, I am a mother having waved a last handkerchief to her oldest child.

My shadow, to my right, lowers my hopes, then raises them, lays them beside me with something of myself inside, small now, a girl. It's a matter of sun, desire, astronomy, a little wind, how my shoes fit, what I've had or not had for breakfast, dreamed in the wee hours as the sun begins to stagger to its feet.

The hand of God is gnarled, bony and veined, like good marble. I used to believe that hand raised above me, giving directions—checkmate, take the pawn, pass. It was all in black and red, or black and white, the players embellished and implacable. There were directions in writing, rules. But so much time has passed since I first read them that I could be one of those headless Greek statues, all stone and hard garment, but the cool air is so pleasing now, here under my arms, and—Ah—my skirt has just blown its silk against my knees.

THE CONTRIBUTORS

SAMUEL ACE is the author of two collections of poetry, *Normal Sex* and *Home in Three Days*, as well as *Don't Wash*, a book and multimedia project with accompanying short video pieces.

KIM ADDONIZIO is the author of four books of poetry, the most recent of which is *What Is This Thing Called Love*.

ROBERT ALEXANDER has published two books of poetry, *What the Raven Said* and *White Pine Sucker River: Poems 1970-1990*, as well as a book of narrative nonfiction about the American Civil War, *Five Forks: Waterloo of the Confederacy*. He edits the Marie Alexander Poetry Series at White Pine Press.

AGHA SHAHID ALI's (1949–2001) books include *Call Me Ishmael Tonight* and *Rooms Are Never Finished*.

JACK ANDERSON is a poet and dance critic. His most recent volume is *Traffic: New and Selected Prose Poems*.

NIN ANDREWS is the author of several books of prose poems, including *Sleeping With Houdini* and *The Book of Orgasms*.

BROTHER ANTHONY OF TAIZE lives in Korea and has translated a number of Korean works into English, including *Eyes of Dew* by Chonggi Mah and *The Depths of a Clam* by Kwang-ku Kim.

RUTH BEHAR's poems have been included in several anthologies. Her most recent book is a memoir, *An Island Called Home: Returning to Jewish Cuba*.

MICHAEL BENEDIKT (1935–2007) authored several collections of prose poetry and poems. He was also the editor of the seminal anthology *The Prose Poem: An International Anthology*.

MARY BERG is a translator from Spanish. Her numerous books of translation include *I've Forgotten Your Name* by Martha Rivera, *The Landscape of Castile* by Antonio Machado, and the forthcoming *The Poet and the Sea* by Juan Ramón Jiménez.

BRUCE BERLIND is a poet and translator of Hungarian. His translations include the work of Agnes Nemes Nagy, Imre Oravecz, and Gyula Illyes.

ROBERT BLY, a seminal figure in American poetry for over fifty years, is the author of numerous books of poetry, prose, and translation. White Pine Press will issue his collected prose poems in 2009.

BETH ARCHER BROMBERT is a translator from the French, and her books include *The Voice of Things* by Francis Ponge.

PAUL CELAN (1920–1970) was one of the major poets of 20th century Europe. Though he wrote mainly in Geman, these selections are from a group of prose poems written in Romanian.

RENÉ CHAR (1907–1988) A major French poet, White Pine published *This Smoke That Carried Us: Selected Poems* in 2004.

MAXINE CHERNOFF has published several collections of poetry and fiction. Her most recent volume of poetry is *Among the Names*.

KIM CHINQUEE is the author of the newly released *Oh Baby: Flash Fictions and Prose Poetry*.

KILLARNEY CLARY is the author of three books of poetry, most recently *Potential Stranger*.

PETER CONNERS is the author of the recently-released book of prose poems, *Of Whiskey & Winter* and a book of fiction, *Emily Ate the Wind*.

ALEŠ DEBELJAK lives in Ljubljana, Slovenia, and is the author of a number of books of poetry and essays. Among his works in English translation are *Anxious Moments* and *The City and the Child*.

SUSANNE DUBROFF is a poet and translator. Her translations include *This Smoke That Carried Us* by René Char.

STUART DYBEK is the author of two collections of poetry, most recently *Streets in Their Own Ink,* and is also the author of several works of fiction.

RUSSELL EDSON is one of the foremost writers of the prose poem and has published twelve collections including *The Tunnel* and *The Rooster's Wife*.

MARY FEENEY translates from the French and worked with the late poet William Matthews on the translations of the French poet Jean Follain.

JEAN FOLLAIN (1903–1971) was a major 20th century French poet. The work included here is from *Dreaming the Miracle: Three French Prose Poets*.

ROBIN FULTON, a British poet and translator, has lived in Norway for many years. He has translated many of the major poets of Norway and Sweden. His most recent collection is *The Great Enigma: Collected Poems of Tomaz Tranströmer*.

VAL GERSTLE's work has appeared in *Cincinnati Poetry Review, Bellingham Review, Louisville Review,* and over forty other publications.

MAUREEN GIBBON is the author of *Magdalena*, a recent volume in the Marie Alexander Poetry Series, and a novel, *Swimming Sweet Arrow*.

GARY GILDNER's most recent books include *The Birthday Party* and *The Bunker in the Parsley Fields*.

RAY GONZALEZ is the author of a number of books of poetry and prose, including the recent *Consideration of the Guitar: New and Selected Poems.*

MIRIAM GOODMAN is the author of *Expense Report* and *Commercial Traveler* among other books of poetry.

S. C. HAHN lives on a farm in southern Sweden, and his poems have appeared in a number of magazines.

MARIE HARRIS, New Hampshire Poet Laureate 1999-2004, is the author of four books of poetry, the most recent of which is *Your Sun, Manny: A Prose Poem Memoir.*

JIM HARRISON is widely-known as a fiction writer, and he has also published numerous volumes of poetry, most recently *Saving Daylight.*

JENNIFER L. HOLLEY has published poetry in several literary magazines.

BROOKE HORVATH is the author of two books of poetry, including *Consolation at Ground Zero* and the recent book of nonfiction, *Understanding Nelson Algren.*

JI-WOO HWANG has published seven books of poems in his native Korea. His first book in English translation is *Even Birds Leave the World.*

HOLLY IGLESIAS's books include *Souvenirs of a Shrunken World* and *Hands-on Saints.* She is also the author of *Boxing Inside the Box: Women's Prose Poetry.*

DAVID IGNATOW (1914–1997) was an early advocate of the prose poem. His books include *Against All Evidence: Selected Poems.*

MARIA (GIACHETTI) JACKETTI is a poet and translator. Her books include *Black Diamond Madonna* and translations of Pablo Neruda and Gabriela Mistral.

MAX JACOB (1876–1944) was a major 20th century French poet. The work included here is from *Dreaming the Miracle: Three French Prose Poets.*

SIBYL JAMES's books include *The Adventures of Stout Mama* and *In China with Harpo and Karl.*

LOUIS JENKINS's most recent books include *North of the Cities* and *Sea Smoke.*

JUAN RAMÓN JIMÉNEZ won the Nobel Prize for literature in 1956. These poems are from the forthcoming translation *The Poet and the Sea.*

JIM JOHNSON is the Duluth poet laureate and is the author of five books including *The Co-op Label.*

PETER JOHNSON is the author of three books of prose poems: *Pretty Happy!*, *Miracles and Mortifications,* and *Eduardo & I.* In addition, he was the editor of the essential journal, *The Prose Poem: An International Journal.*

MAURICE KENNY is the author of many books of poetry, fiction, and essays.

His most recent books include *Connotations* and a reissue of his award-winning collection *The Mama Poems*.

WON-CHUNG KIM is a translator from and into Korean. His English translations include *Heart's Agony* by Chiha Kim and *Even Birds Leave the World* by Ji-woo Hwang.

MARY A. KONCEL's books include *You Can Tell the Horse Anything* and *Closer to Day*.

MARIA KÖRÖSY has prepared literal versions of many Hungarian poets. She holds a Master of Arts in English from the University of Budapest.

WILLIAM KULIK is a translator from the French. His books include *The Voice* by Robert Desnos and *The Selected Poems of Max Jacob*.

KIM KWANG-KYU has published eight collection of poetry. *The Depths of a Clam: Selected Poems* is his first volume in English.

NANCY LAGOMARSINO is the author of three books of prose poetry, *Sleep Handbook*, *The Secretary Parables*, and *Light from an Eclipse*.

JAY LEEMING is the author of *Dynamite on a China Plate*.

LARRY LEVIS's (1946–1996) books include *Elegy* and *The Selected Levis*.

P. H. LIOTTA's most recent book of poems is *The Graveyard of Fallen Monuments*.

GIAN LOMBARDO's books include *Of All the Corners to Forget* and *Who Lets Go First*.

CHONGGI MAH is the author of numerous volume of poetry in his native Korea but has lived most of his adult life in the U.S. working as a doctor. *Eyes of Dew* is his first collection in English.

DENNIS MALONEY's most recent books include *The Map is not the Territory* and a translation of *The Landscape of Castile* by Antonio Machado. He is the founding editor/publisher of White Pine Press.

MORTON MARCUS is a prolific author. His most recent books include *Pursuing the Dream Bone* (prose poetry) and *Striking Through the Masks: A Literary Memoir*.

PETER MARKUS's most recent books include *The Singing Fish* and *Bob, or Man on Boat: A Novel*.

WILLIAM MATTHEWS (1942–1997) was the author of eleven books of poetry, including *Search Party: Collected Poems*.

KATHLEEN McGOOKEY's most recent book is *Whatever Shines*, which is included in the Marie Alexander Poetry Series.

MICHAEL McGRIFF is a poet and translator. His book *Dismantling the Hills* won the 2007 Agnes Lynch Starrett Poetry Prize.

MARTIN MCKINSEY is a translator from Greek and his books include *Late Into the Night: Last Poems of Yannis Ritos, Acropolis,* and *Tram: Poems of Nikos Engonopoulos.*

JAY MEEK is the author of *Trains in Winter, Windows, The Memphis Letters,* and other books.

CHRISTOPHER MERRILL is a prolific author and translator. His most recent book of poetry is *Brilliant Water.*

LAWRENCE MILLMAN is the author of *Northern Latitudes, Last Places: A Journey in the North, Our Like Will Not Be Here Again,* and other works.

GABRIELA MISTRAL is the only Latin American woman to receive the Nobel prize for Literature. Her works in English include *A Gabriela Mistral Reader* and a book of *recados* titled *Women.*

PABLO NERUDA (1904–1973) won the Nobel Prize for Literature in 1971. He is regarded as one of the greatest poets of the 20th century.

KRISTY NIELSEN is the author of *Two Girls,* a book of prose poems, and an electronic chapbook from Web del Sol.

NAOMI SHIHAB NYE is a well-known poet whose works include *Fuel* and the forthcoming *You and Yours.*

NINA NYHART is the author of two books of poetry, *Openers* and *French for Soldiers.*

TOMMY OLOFSSON is a Swedish poet and translator. *Elemental Poems* is his first volume in English translation.

IMRE ORAVECZ is the author of five books in his native Hungary. *When You Became She* is his only book in English.

JEAN PEARSON is a poet and translator. Her books include *On Speaking Terms with Earth,* and *Elemental Poems* by Tommy Oloffson, a translation from the Swedish.

ROBERT PERCHAN's books include *Overdressed to Kill* and *Fluid in Darkness, Frozen in Light.*

FRANCIS PONGE (1899–1988) was a major 20th century French poet. The work included here is from *Dreaming the Miracle: Three French Prose Poets.*

CRISTIAN POPESCU has published three books of poetry in his native Romania.

YANNIS RITSOS (1909–1990) was one of the important poets of modern Greece.

VERN RUTSALA's recent volumes include *The Moment's Equation, A Handbook for*

Writers: New and Selected Prose Poems, and *Little-Known Sports.*

BARRY SILESKY is the author of *The Disease: Poems* and *John Gardner: Literary Outlaw.*

AMELA SIMIC is a translator from Bosnian and has translated Goran Simic's *From Sarejevo with Sorrow* and *Immigrant Blues.*

CHARLES SIMIC, a former Poet Laureate of the United States, is the author of numerous volumes, most recently *Sixty Poems* and *The Little Something.*

GORAN SIMIC is the author of *Immigrant Blues, From Sarajevo with Sorrow,* and *Yesterday's People.*

LENNART SJÖGREN is the author of over twenty collections of poetry in Swedish.

WILLIAM SLAUGHTER is the author of *The Politics of My Heart* and *Untold Stories.*

THOMAS R. SMITH is the author of several volumes of poetry, most recently *Waking Before Dawn* and *Winter Hours.*

ADAM SORKIN has translated over twenty-five books of contemporary Romanian literature, including *Chaosmos* by Magda Carneci.

MADELON SPRENGNETHER is the author of many books, including *The Angel of Duluth, The Normal Heart,* and *Crying at the Movies: A Film Memoir.*

MAURA STANTON is the author of five books of poetry, most recently *Glacier Wine,* and her most recent book of fiction is *Cities in the Sea.*

BOGDAN STEFANESCU has translated Romanian works into English and many British and American writers into Romanian.

EVA STRÖM trained and worked as a doctor before becoming a full-time writer. She is the author of several books of poetry and prose in Swedish.

JAMES TATE is the author of a number of books of poetry, including *Return to the City of White Donkeys* and *The Ghost Soldiers.*

CARINE TOPAL's books include *God As Thief* and *Bed of Want.*

ALISON TOWNSEND is the author of the forthcoming *Persephone in America,* as well as *The Blue Dress* and *What the Body Knows.*

TOMAS TRANSTRÖMER is one of Sweden's most well-known poets. His most recent book in English is *The Great Enigma: New Collected Poems.*

MARK TURSI is the author of *The Impossible Picic.*

MARK VINZ is the author of several books of poems, including *Long Distance.* He is a co-editor of the prose poem anthology, *The Party Train.*

LIZ WALDNER is the author of several books of poetry including *Dark Would (the missing person)* and *Saving the Appearances.*

Rosmarie Waldrop is a noted poet and translator. Her most recent book is *Curves to the Apple*.

Charles Harper Webb's books include the recent *Hot Popsicles* and the award-winning *Liver*.

Tom Whalen's books include *Winter Coat, Roithamer's Universe*, and the recent chapbook *Dolls*.

Peter Wortsman is the author of *A Modern Way to Die* and the translator of *Travel Pictures* by Heinrich Heine and *Posthumous Papers of a Living Author* by Robert Musil.

James Wright (1927–1980) was one of the significant American poets of the 20th century. His books include *A Wild Perfection: Selected Letters, Above the River: The Complete Poems*, and *The Shape of Light*.

David Young's books of poetry include *Black Lab* and *At The White Window*.

Gary Young's most recent books include *No Other Life* and *Pleasure*.

Genie Zeiger is the author of several books of poetry, including *Leaving Egypt* and *Radio Waves*. She is also the author of two memoirs, *Atta Girl* and *How I Find Her*.

Clark Zlotchew is a writer and translator. He has translated the work of Julio Luis Borges, Pablo Neruda, and Julio Ricci.

Prose Poetry Anthologies since 1995

Always the Beautiful Answer: A Prose Poem Primer. Edited by Ruth Moon Kempher. St. Augustine, FL: Kings Estate Press, 1999.

The Best of the Prose Poem: An International Journal. Edited by Peter Johnson. Buffalo, NY: White Pine Press, 2000.

BLINK: Flash Fiction Before You Can Bat an Eye. Edited by Wanda Wade Mukherjee. The Paper Journey Press, 2006.

A Curious Architecture: A Selection of Contemporary Prose Poems. Edited by Rupert Loydell and David Miller. Exeter, UK: Stride Publications, 1996.

Flash Fiction Forward: 80 Very Short Stories. Edited by James Thomas and Robert Shapard. New York: W. W. Norton, 2006.

Freedom to Breathe: Modern Prose Poetry From Baudelaire to Pinter. Edited by Geoffrey Godbert. Exeter, UK: Stride Publications, 2002.

Great American Prose Poems: From Poe to the Present. Edited by David Lehman. New York: Scribner, 2003.

Micro Fiction: An Anthology of Really Short Stories. Edited by Jerome Stern. New York: W. W. Norton, 1996.

Models of the Universe: An Anthology of the Prose Poem. Edited by Stuart Friebert and David Young. Oberlin, OH: Oberlin College Press, 1995.

New Sudden Fiction: Short-Short Stories from America and Beyond. Edited by Robert Shapard and James Thomas. New York: W .W. Norton, 2007.

No Boundaries: Prose Poems by 24 American Poets. Edited by Ray Gonzalez. Dorset, VT: Tupelo Press, 2003.

The Party Train: A Collection of North American Prose Poetry. Edited by Robert Alexander, Mark Vinz, and C. W. Truesdale. Minneapolis, MN: New

Rivers Press, 1996.

PP/FF: An Anthology. Edited by Peter Conners. Buffalo, NY: Starcherone Books, 2006.

Sudden Fiction (Continued): 60 New Short-Short Stories. Edited by Robert Shapard and James Thomas. New York: W. W. Norton, 1996.

Suddenly: Prose Poetry and Sudden Fiction. Edited by Jackie Pelham. Houston, TX: Martin House, 1998.

Sudden Stories: The Mammoth Book of Miniscule Fiction. Edited by Dinty W. Moore. Mammoth Press, 2003.

The World's Shortest Stories: Murder, Love, Horror, Suspense. Edited by Steve Moss. Philadelphia, PA: Running Press Book Publishers, 1998.

The World's Shortest Stories of Love and Death: Passion, Betrayal, Suspicion, Revenge. Edited by Steve Moss and John M. Daniel. Philadelphia, PA: Running Press Book Publishers, 2000.

Compiled by Mark Tursi

ACKNOWLEDGMENTS
(This is an extension of the copyright page.)

Work by the following authors is reprinted from *The Best of the Prose Poem: An International Journal*, copyright 2000 by Providence College, published by *The Prose Poem: An International Journal* and White Pine Press, with the permission of Peter Johnson and the authors:

Samuel Ace, Kim Addonizio, Agha Shahid Ali, Nin Andrews, Ruth Behar, Michael Benedikt, Maxine Chernoff, Killarney Clary, Stuart Dybek, Russell Edson, Val Gerstle, Gary Gildner, Ray Gonzalez, Miriam Goodman, S. C. Hahn, Jennifer L. Holley, Brooke Horvath, Holly Inglesias, David Ignatow, Sibyl James, Louis Jenkins, Jim Johnson, Mary A. Koncel, Larry Levis, P .H. Liotta , Gian Lombardo, Peter Markus, Jay Meek, Kristy Nielsen, Naomi Shihab Nye, Nina Nyhart, Imre Oravecz, Robert Perchan, Cristian Poepescu, Yannis Ritos, Barry Silesky, Charles Simic, Goran Simic, William Slaughter, Thomas R. Smith, Maura Stanton, James Tate, Carine Topal, Mark Vinz, Liz Waldner, Rosemary Waldrop, Charles Harper Webb, Tom Whalen, Peter Wortsman, David Young, Gary Young, and translators Bruce Berlind, Maria Korosy, Adam Sorkin, Bogdan Stefanescu, Martin McKinsey, Amela Simic, and Christopher Merrill.

Harris, Marie. "Louis Antoine de Bougainville" in *The Party Train: A Collection of North American Prose Poetry*. Mineapolis, MN: New Rivers Press, 1996. Reprinted by permission of the author.

Leeming, Jay. *Dynamite on a China Plate*. Omaha, NE: Backwaters Press, 2006. Reprinted by permission of the author.

Maloney, Dennis. *The Map is Not the Territory*. Greensboro, NC: Unicorn Press, 1990. Used by permission of the author.

The following authors' work is reprinted from the following volumes published by White Pine Press, Buffalo, NY, and is used with the permission of White Pine Press:

Robert Alexander, *What the Raven Said*, copyright 2006

The Marie Alexander Poetry Series

Series Editor: Robert Alexander

Volme 11
The House of Your Dream:
An International Collection of Prose Poetry
Edited by Robert Alexander and Dennis Maloney

Volume 10
Magdalena
Maureen Gibbon

Volume 9
The Angel of Duluth
Madelon Sprengnether

Volume 8
Light from an Eclipse
Nancy Lagomarsino

Volume 7
A Handbook for Writers
Vern Rutsala

Volume 6
The Blue Dress
Alison Townsend